The Internet and the World Wide Web for Teachers

Second Edition

Eugene F. Provenzo, Jr.

University of Miami

Allyn & Bacon

Boston London Toronto Sydney Tokyo Singapore

For Arlene Brett,
Friend, co-author, colleague—
in appreciation of many years of sharing, learning, and teaching.

Copyright © 2002 by Allyn & Bacon
A Pearson Education Company
160 Gould Street
Needham Heights, Massachusetts 02494-2130
www.ablongman.com

Book design by Eugene F. Provenzo, Jr.

The images on pages 4, 8, 11, 30, 39, 44, 48, 73, 77, 78, 83, 84, 90, 91 (top and
bottom), 92, 93, 94, 95, 117, 121, 122, 123, and 129 were obtained from IMSI
Master Clips/Master Photos © Collection, 1895 Francisco Blvd. East San Rafael,
CA 94901-5506. Images on pages 18, 43, 46, 47, 49, 50, 52, 55, 59, 60, 65, 69,
71, 72 (top and bottom), 75, 82, 84, 90, 92, 94, 102, 103, 108, 109, 110, 111,
114, 116, 118, 130, 131, 132, 135, and 136 were obtained from volumes
included in the Dover *Pictorial Archive* series, Dover Publications, Inc., 31 East
2nd Street, Mineola, N.Y. 11501. Permission to use the web site banner on page
3 was provided through the courtesy of the National Council for Accreditation of
teachers. The web site banner on page 20 is used with permission from Kathy
Schrock. Use of the web banner on page 113 and the illustration on page 114 is
with the permission of Curriculum Associates, Incorporated, North Bellerica,
Massachusetts 01862. The images on page 7 (bottom), 13, 14, 15, 16, 17, 19,
21, 22, 23, 24, 25, 26, 27, 31, 32, 34, 35, 37, 49, 50, 54, 55, 56, 58, 63, 64, 65,
66, 67, 69, 70, 71, 75, 76, 77, 79, 80, 81, 82, 83, 85, 87, 88, 89, 91, 97, 98, 100,
101, 102, 104, 107, 108, 117, 118, 119, 128, and 138 were obtained from *Art
Explosionl,* Nova Development, 1995-98.

ISBN 0-205-34349-X
Printed in the United States of America
10 9 8 7 6 5 4 3 2 1   03 02 01

Contents

Preface

This is the second edition of *The Internet and World Wide Web for Teachers*. It incorporates many of the elements of the first edition, while expanding its content to reflect changes in the web since the book's first publication. The purpose of the book remains the same: (1) to provide its readers with a guide to using the World Wide Web as part of their studies in education; and (2) to show them how this remarkable technology can change traditional teaching and the way people work and learn in schools.

While this book includes chapters for those with no experience using the Internet and the World Wide Web, it can also be used by those of you who have a reasonably high level of computer literacy and, more specifically, already know how to use the Internet and the World Wide Web.

Ideally, you will use this book in the first course in a college or university's education sequence. At the University of Miami, where the author teaches, for example, it is used as a supplemental text for the Introduction to Education Course, which has an extensive web-based component built into its curriculum. It could also be used in the one-credit introductory course on computing and education that we offer in the same semester as our Introduction to Education course.

Other instructors and institutions may find this a useful text for general introduction to computing courses or as a supplement for courses such as Educational Psychology, Reading in the Content Area, or General Curriculum Methods.

Introducing this book into the traditional four-year education curriculum as early as possible will provide students with a useful resource that they can take advantage of throughout their undergraduate studies. Although the emphasis is on using the book in the student's work in education, its potential for use in other university coursework should be clear. Chapter Eight, "Using the Web as a Resource for Courses Outside of Your Studies in Education," focuses on this issue.

I would like to thank the many people who have contributed to the development of this project. First and foremost are my undergraduates and graduate students at the University of Miami who have helped me better understand how the Internet can be used in both undergraduate and K–12 instruction. In particular Liana Chiappone has provided help and insight on creative uses of curriculum and the Internet. Alan Whitney and his computer staff in the School of Education Angelo Corbo, Joel Soulders and Victor Rodriquez), Bill Vilberg in the Instructional Advancement Center, University of Miami, Arlene Brett, Gil Cuevas and Chuck Mangrum are also thanked for their ideas and support. My wife, Asterie Baker Provenzo, carefully edited both the first draft of this book and this new edition. I thank her for her constant help and encouragement. Thanks to my department chair Jeanne Shay Schumm for providing a creative and caring environment in which to conduct my day-to-day work. Finally, I would like to thank Dean Sam Yarger at the School of Education, University of Miami, for his ongoing support and encouragement—support and encouragement that has allowed us to develop significant new directions in our undergraduate and graduate programs that I am convinced not only represent the cutting edge in education but provide us a glimpse of the future of education in the decades ahead.

Eugene F. Provenzo, Jr.
University of Miami

Web Site

A web site for this book can be found at:

The Internet and the World Wide Web for Teachers
www.ablongman.com/provenzo2e

While this book with its ideas and web addresses can stand on its own, you may find the web site for this book extremely helpful, particularly as you begin your own explorations of the World Wide Web and cyberspace.

At the web site you will find links to all of the sites listed in this book, as well as to other resources that will help you take advantage of the Internet and the World Wide Web and its resources. The author and the publisher will attempt to keep up the addresses at the web site, but please keep in mind that the Internet and the World Wide Web are a fluid and constantly changing medium. Web sites come and go, and as they do, addresses and links become outdated.

Finally, for those who are new to this subject, please note that Internet and computer definitions are defined in the Glossary at the end of this book.

Chapter One

The Internet and the World Wide Web for Educators

Education as a professional field is constantly changing. Changes in values take place, new curriculums are introduced, and new technologies redefine how we teach and learn. The most interesting and important innovation in education in recent years is the widespread introduction of computers into the schools. Computers represent powerful tools that can be used by both students and teachers for instructional purposes. Of particular interest are the Internet and more specifically, the World Wide Web, which is radically redefining how we obtain information and the way we teach and learn. The world can literally be brought into the schoolhouse.

This book provides an introduction and guide for teachers to the Internet and the World Wide Web. It is intended to help teachers not only use the Internet and its resources in their own education but to integrate them into their work as teachers. Before you begin, you may wonder: Do I really need to be skilled at using computers and the Internet and the World Wide Web to be a good teacher?

The answer is yes—without a doubt! The National Council for the Accreditation of Teacher Education (NCATE), the main teacher education accreditation group in the United States, argues that when it comes to computers, all teachers need to develop: new understandings, new approaches, new roles, new forms of professional development, and new attitudes.

NCATE's Requirements for the "New Professional Teacher"
(Source: *Technology and the New Professional Teacher: Preparing for the 21st Century Classroom* [1997])

New Understandings

Teachers need to understand the deep impact technology is having on society as a whole: how technology has changed the nature of work and communication and our understanding of the development of knowledge.

New Approaches

Today, teachers must recognize that information is available from sources that go well beyond textbooks and teachers—mass media, communities, etc.—and help students understand and make use of the many ways in which they can gain access to information. Teachers must employ a wide range of technological tools and software as part of their own instructional repertoire.

New Roles

Teachers should help students pursue their own inquiries, making use of technologies to find, organize, and interpret information and to become reflective and critical about information quality and sources.

New Forms of Professional Development

Teachers must participate in formal courses, some of which may be delivered in nontraditional ways, e.g., via telecommunications; they must also become part of ongoing, informal learning communities with other professionals who share their interests and concerns.

New Attitudes

Finally, teachers need an attitude that is fearless in the use of technology, encourages them to take risks, and inspires them to become lifelong learners. (*Ibid.*)

National Council for the Accreditation of Teacher Education
http://www.ncate.org/

Technology and the New Professional Teacher: Preparing for the 21st Century Classroom (1997)
http://www.ncate.org/accred/projects/tech/tech-21.htm

In NCATE's report *Technology and the New Professional Teacher: Preparing for the 21st Century Classroom*, brief case studies demonstrate the innovative use of technology in teacher education programs. You can access these case studies at:

NCATE Case Studies of Technology Use in Teacher Education
http://www.ncate.org/accred/projects/tech/caseintro.htm

A list of technology themes included in NCATE's current standards can be found at:

Technology Themes in NCATE's Current Standards
http://www.ncate.org/accred/projects/tech/current.htm

Other groups such as the International Society for the Study of Technology and Education have also established national standards in the use of technology for both K-12 students and for teachers. These standards, while much more detailed and comprehensive than those provided by NCATE, are concerned with many of the same issues.

http://www.iste.org/

International Society for the Study of Technology and Education's *National Standards for Teachers* (2000):

I. TECHNOLOGY OPERATIONS AND CONCEPTS.

Teachers demonstrate a sound understanding of technology operations and concepts. Teachers:

A. demonstrate introductory knowledge, skills, and understanding of concepts related to technology.

B. demonstrate continual growth in technology knowledge and skills to stay abreast of current and emerging technologies.

II. PLANNING AND DESIGNING LEARNING ENVIRONMENTS AND EXPERIENCES.

Teachers plan and design effective learning environments and experiences supported by technology. Teachers:

A. design developmentally appropriate learning opportunities that apply technology-enhanced instructional strategies to support the diverse needs of learners.

B. apply current research on teaching and learning with technology when planning learning environments and experiences.

C. identify and locate technology resources and evaluate them for accuracy and suitability.

D. plan for the management of technology resources within the context of learning activities.

E. plan strategies to manage student learning in a technology-enhanced environment.

III. TEACHING, LEARNING, AND THE CURRICULUM.

Teachers implement curriculum plans, that include methods and strategies for applying technology to maximize student learning. Teachers:

A. facilitate technology-enhanced experiences that address content standards and student technology standards.

B. use technology to support learner-centered strategies that address the diverse needs of students.

C. apply technology to develop students' higher order skills and creativity.

D. manage student learning activities in a technology-enhanced environment.

IV. ASSESSMENT AND EVALUATION.

Teachers apply technology to facilitate a variety of effective assessment and evaluation strategies. Teachers:

A. apply technology in assessing student learning of subject matter using a variety of assessment techniques.

B. use technology resources to collect and analyze data, interpret results, and communicate findings to improve instructional practice and maximize student learning.

C. apply multiple methods of evaluation to determine students' appropriate use of technology resources for learning, communication,and productivity.

V. PRODUCTIVITY AND PROFESSIONAL PRACTICE.

Teachers use technology to enhance their productivity and professional practice. Teachers:

A. use technology resources to engage in ongoing professional development and lifelong learning.

B. continually evaluate and reflect on professional practice to make informed decisions regarding the use of technology in support of student learning.

C. apply technology to increase productivity.

D. use technology to communicate and collaborate with peers, parents, and the larger community in order to nurture student learning.

VI. SOCIAL, ETHICAL, LEGAL, AND HUMAN ISSUES.

Teachers understand the social, ethical, legal, and human issues surrounding the use of technology in PK-12 schools and apply those principles in practice. Teachers:

A. model and teach legal and ethical practice related to technology use.

B. apply technology resources to enable and empower learners with diverse backgrounds, characteristics, and abilities.

C. identify and use technology resources that affirm diversity.

D. promote safe and healthy use of technology resources.

E. facilitate equitable access to technology resources for all students.

The ISTE's standards for K-12 students are available at:

National Education Technology Standards for Students
http://cnets.iste.org/index2ss.html

The ISTE's standards for teachers are available at:

National Education Technology Standards for Teachers
http://cnets.iste.org/index3.html

In its discussions of teacher standards and computers both NCATE and ISTE are talking about a wide range of technologies that have an impact on schools and teachers. Of all of the new technologies, the Internet and the World Wide Web seem to hold the greatest promise for transforming traditional teaching and learning. Let's begin to examine why the Internet and the World Wide Web are so important.

Why are the Internet and the World Wide Web Important for Education?

The Internet and the World Wide Web are important to a field like education for many reasons. I believe the most significant reason is that the Internet brings a massive set of information resources into the classroom that have never been available before. Students can easily visit web sites around the world. No matter how isolated or poor, a child with a connection to the Internet and the World Wide Web can have access to the great museums and libraries of the world. The Louvre Museum in Paris, the Library of Congress in Washington, DC, or the Victoria and Albert Museum in London is literally just a computer with browser program and modem, a telephone connection, and mouse-click or two away.

Musee du Louvre
http://www.paris.org:80/Musees/Louvre/

The Library of Congress
http://lcweb.loc.gov/homepage/lchp.html

The Victoria and Albert Museum
http://www.vam.ac.uk/

Students can have access to web sites that not only provide them with background about our history, but also our politics. The American Memory Project at the Library of the Congress, for example, includes literally millions of photographs, documents, sound files and even movies from our past—all of them available online.

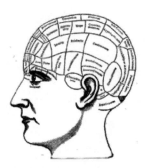

American Memory Project
http://memory.loc.gov/

At the National Archives you can find thousands of documents (including the Constitution and the Declaration of Independence), photographs and even posters.

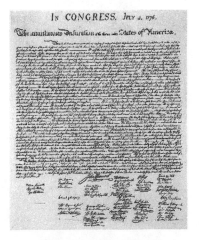

National Archives
http://www.nara.gov/

You can visit the White House web site, learn about its history, and even take a virtual tour of its rooms.

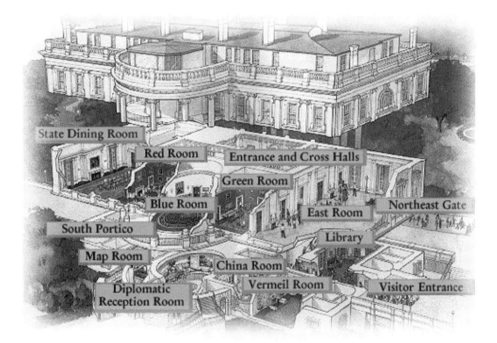

White House
http://www.whitehouse.gov/

Other places important to our government such as the House of Representatives, the Senate and the Supreme Court can also be visited online.

Congress.Org
http://www.congress.org/

United States Senate
http://www.senate.gov/

Supreme Court of the United States
http://www.supremecourtus.gov/

A gateway to the Smithsonian Institution and its extraordinary collections of history, art, technology and natural history can be found at:

The Smithsonian
http://www.si.edu

NASA Quest provides teachers with extensive curriculums on space exploration and the history of the flight. Programs such as the Space Team Online website provides teachers and students with biographies of NASA scientists and information about their work, an e-mail service for answering individual questions, lesson plans, collaborative publishing projects for students, and chat rooms where teachers can meet one another and exchange ideas and information.

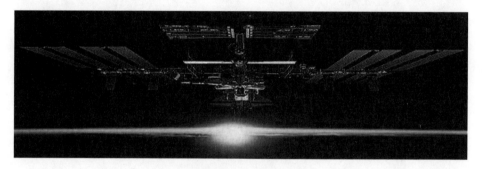

NASA Quest
http://quest.arc.nasa.gov/

Extraordinary public domain images of photographs and videos in the NASA archive can be accessed at:

NASA Multimedia Archives
http://www.nasa.gov/hqpao/library.html/

Even the surface of the planet Mars and the outer reaches of the Solar System can be explored by a student with an internet connection, a modem and an inexpensive computer.

Mars Pathfinder
http://mars.jpl.nasa.gov/MPF/index1.html

Not only can you wander through the great museums of the world via the Internet, but you can also exchange scientific research data with students across the country and even talk to scientists by e-mail in remote locations of the world. Project Jason, for example, has students connect with scientists for e-mail exchanges in a wide range of fields, as well as across a wide range of disciplines ranging from biology, to ecology, to oceanography. As part of Project Jason, students learn about the scientists they are connecting to and the type of work they do. Dr. Debbie K. Steinberg, for example, is one of the Jason IX Expedition scientists. A researcher and member of the faculty at the Bermuda Biological Station for Research, she describes her mission for the Jason IX expedition as being "to demonstrate the excitement and ecological importance of doing oceanographic research. I hope students will gain an appreciation for the incredible diversity of organisms, in particular the plankton, that live in the sea. My goal is to facilitate understanding of the structure of the ocean and communities it supports, how organisms 'make a living' in the open sea, and how organisms affect cycling of elements. I want students to gain an appreciation for how oceanographic research is done, and to show how the oceans affect our daily lives, whether through climate, production of food, or in other ways."

Project Jason
http://seawifs.gsfc.nasa.gov/JASON.html

Dr. Deborah K. Steinberg's Chat Transcript (Jason IX Expedition)

December 18, 1997

Todd: Hello everyone and welcome to the chat session!

Todd: I'm Todd and I'll be your moderator today.

Todd: I can see that some people are starting to file into the auditorium.

Jude: Hello Leaguers!

Todd: Dr. Steinberg is here on stage with us. That chat will start in about 5 minutes.

Todd: If you have questions for Dr. Steinberg, you can start submitting them now.

Todd: Be sure to type /ask to start your question

Todd: I'm getting LOTS of questions from the Leaguers (Keep 'em coming!). Does anyone else have a question?

Dr. Steinberg: ready!

Todd: You can submit your questions by typing /ask

Todd: Hi Dr. Steinberg. This is Todd. I'll be your moderator today. We're starting to get lots of good questions.

Todd: I'll present the questions to you. Here we go....

Leaguers5: When did you decide to become a scientist?

Dr. Steinberg: I think it was when I was about 12 years old and went diving on a coral reef for the first time, I was always interested in the sea though, ever since I was a kid growing up near the Chesapeake Bay.

David Malmquist: What is marine snow?

Douglas School: What does marine snow look like?

Dr. Steinberg: Marine snow is aggregates of detritus in the sea, it is made up of dead phytoplankton (tiny algae), mucus secreted by zooplankton (tiny animals). It also contains a number of live creatures that live in the particle. These tiny bacteria, and also little crustaceans (zooplankton) use the marine snow as a habitat and food source.

You can also have electronic pen pals in foreign countries, exchange electronic letters with them, and even conduct different types of research projects with one another—all via the Internet.

Friends and Partners
http://solar.rtd.utk.edu/friends/home.html

Using the Internet and the World Wide Web, you can literally tour the world while seated in front of your computer. The web site Cammunity.com, for example, allows you to link to over 10,000 live web cameras around the world. You can explore a street in Paris, ride with a taxi cab driver in New York City, or discover an ocean reef off the coast of Australia.

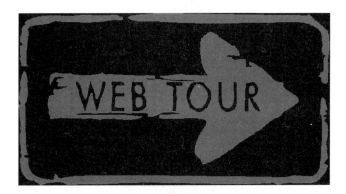

Cammunity.Com
www.cammunity.com

An extraordinary multiple-view series web camera can be linked to at:

Times Square Cam
http://www.earthcam.com/usa/newyork/timessquare/

Sites such as the Getty Museum's Arts Ed Net are providing resources for teachers to introduce art and art history activities in their classrooms.

Arts Ed Net
http://www.artsednet.getty.edu/

More informal art sites for teachers and kids include:

The Incredible Art Department
http://www.artswire.org/kenroar/

Mark Kistler's Imagination Station
http://www.draw3d.com/

By downloading web-based audio files you can listen to the voices of ex-slaves describing their lives before they and their families were freed, or you can hear what it was like to come through Ellis Island as an immigrant.

Index of Slave Narratives, University of Virginia Hypertext Library
http://xroads.virginia.edu/~HYPER/wpa/index.html

Ellis Island—Through America's Gateway
http://www.i-channel.com/ellis/index.html

Resources on contemporary and popular culture can be found at:

Alt.Culture
http://www.altculture.com/cgi-bin/home.cgi

Popcultures.Com
http://www.altculture.com/cgi-bin/home.cgi

Information on foreign countries can be found at many different sites including:

The Electronic Embassy (Embassies in Washington, D.C.)
http://www.embassy.org/

United Nations
http://www.un.org/

You can take electronic field trips and tour famous buildings and historical sites with your students at web addresses such as the Tower of London, the Eiffel Tower, the Empire State Building and the Sistine Chapel.

Tower of London
http://www.camelot-group.com/tower/

Eiffel Tower
http://www.tour-eiffel.fr/

Empire State Building
http://www.esbnyc.com/

Sistine Chapel
http://www.christusrex.org/www1/sistine/0-Tour.html

There are numerous "gateway sites" available from the government and through private agencies that can help you find web sites and information that is of interest to you. The Federal Web locator, for example, provides a general guide to almost all Federal Government information found on the Internet.

FedWorld Information Network
http://www.fedworld.gov/

The main gateway for web sites sponsored by the Federal government for the Executive branch is:

Federal Government Web Sites of the Executive Branch
http://lcweb.loc.gov/global/executive/fed.html

Similar types of gateways can also be found in specialized subject areas such as science.

Science Education Gateway
http://cse.ssl.berkeley.edu/segway/

Perhaps the best gateway site available in the Humanities is the Voice of the Shuttle:

Voice of the Shuttle
http://vos.ucsb.edu/

Or you can find out what's playing on National Public Radio:

National Public Radio
http://www.npr.org/

Information sources including both general and specialty newspapers and magazines are easily found online. Examples include:

Instructor Magazine
http://teacher.scholastic.com/products/instructor.htm

U. S. News and World Report
http://www.usnews.com/usnews/home.htm

T. H. E. Journal (Computers and Education)
http://www.thejournal.com/

Education Week (Newspaper)
http://www.edweek.org/

Extensive resources on ancient literature and culture can be found at the Perseus Project and Project Libellus.

Perseus Project
http://www.perseus.tufts.edu/

Project Libellus
http://osman.classics.washington.edu/libellus/libellus.html

Or museum sites, like the Birch Aquarium at the Scripps Oceanographic Institute and the Monterey Bay Aquarium, are only a click away on the Internet.

Aquarium Museum
http://aqua.ucsd.edu

Monterey Bay Aquarium
http://www.mbayaq.org/

The Internet and the World Wide Web make information and communication resources available to people in ways that are unprecedented. Imagine, for a moment, being a student in a remote rural school in North Carolina or in an inner-city neighborhood in Detroit or Chicago with access to the Internet and the World Wide Web. Reference books that might otherwise be unavailable to you are only a modem connection and a few clicks away.

> "He who wishes to teach us a truth should not tell it to us, but simply suggest it with a brief gesture, a gesture which starts an ideal trajectory in the air along which we glide until we find ourselves at the feet of the new truth."
>
> –José Ortega y Gasset, *Meditations on Quixote* (1914)

Bartlett's Familiar Quotations
http://www.columbia.edu/acis/bartleby/bartlett

Roget's Thesaurus
http://humanities.uchicago.edu/forms_unrest/ROGET.html

Virtual Reference Desk
http://thorplus.lib.purdue.edu/reference/index.html

Webster's Dictionary
http://c.gp.cs.cmu.edu:5103/prog/webster

World Atlas on the Web
http://pubweb.parc.xerox.com/map/

Consider using this almost magical electronic tool to reach out to the world. How does having a tool like this change what and how students learn? How will it change the nature of instruction and the traditional role of the teacher? The World Wide Web provides an almost unlimited set of curricular resources. Not only is information on every imaginable topic available, but lesson plans and strategies for teaching developed by other educators are at your fingertips as well.

Esther Dyson in her book *Release 2.0: A Design for Living in the Digital Age* asks what it is that the Internet can do if schools get the proper equipment and teachers the proper training. According to her:

1. It can help connect teachers and other school personnel—to one another, to parents, and to students.

2. It can connect children—to one another, to teachers, to other sources of information—and perhaps even to their parents.

3. Net-based rating services of various kinds can provide for better schooling from outside. (Dyson, 1998, p. 86)

Many of the most interesting educational web sites are being created by teachers themselves. Kathy Schrock is the District Technology Department Head for the Dennis-Yarmouth Regional School District on Cape Cod, Massachusetts. She has one of the most interesting educational sites on the Internet, which she describes as "a classified list of sites on the Internet found to be useful for enhancing curriculum and teacher professional growth." From her web site you will be able to connect to almost every imaginable type of site about education and teaching to be found on the Internet and the World Wide Web, as well as get information about evaluating web sites, integrating the web into your classroom instruction, and creating home pages for your school.

Kathy Shrock's Guide for Educators
http://www.capecod.net/schrockguide/index.htm

Teachers can find help in introducing technology into their classrooms from many sources. Guides to the innovative work being done by K-12 schools can, for example, be found at Web 66, a project sponsored by the 3-M Corporation and the University of Minnesota School of Education.

Web66
http://web66.coled.umn.edu

Teacher mailing lists and chat rooms make it possible for educators to meet with other colleagues and exchange ideas about their work. Web 66 links teachers who are interested in implementing and managing World Wide Web servers in K-12 schools with one another from around the world.

Web66 and Web66NT Mailing Lists
http://web66.coled.umn.edu/List/Default.html

Sites such as the National School Network, link teachers to valuable resources about integrating computers, the Internet and World Wide Web into their classroom instruction.

National School Network
http://nsn.bbn.com/

Another chat room that provides teachers the opportunity to discuss their educational interests and needs is:

Teacher Talk
http://www.mightymedia.com/talk/working.htm

A site devoted specifically to teachers helping each other in their work and exchanging ideas is:

Teachers Helping Teachers
http://www.pacificnet.net/~mandel/

The web sites of professional organizations such as the National Education Association and the American Federation of Teachers can be visited, as well as state and federal organizations concerned with educational issues and research.

American Federation of Teachers
http://www.aft.org/index.htm

National Education Association
http://www.nea.org/

American Educational Research Association
http://aera.net/

Teachers using the Internet and the World Wide Web can visit web sites supported by their individual state departments of education. Nearly every state has a web site with resources of its own, as well as links to related web sites. State Department of Education sites are excellent places to find out about certification, grants and project monies, or to check out a specialized curriculum area (state history).

State Department of Education Web Sites

Alabama
http://www.alsde.edu

Alaska
http://www.educ.state.ak.us/

Arizona
http://ade.state.az.us/

Arkansas
http://arkedu.k12.ar.us

California
http://goldmine.cde.ca.gov.

Colorado
http://cde.state.co.us/

Delaware
http://www.dpi.state.de.us/dpi/index.html

Florida
http://www.firn.edu/doe/index.html

Georgia
http://gadoe.gac.peachnet.edu/

Hawaii
http://www.K12.hi.us/

Idaho
http://www.state.id.us/

Illinois
http://www.isbe.state.il.us/homepage.html

Kansas
http://www.ksbe.state.ks.us/

Kentucky
http://www.kde.state.ky.us/

Louisiana
http://www.doe.state.la.us/

Maryland
http://www.mec.state.md.us/mec/

Massachusetts
http://info.doe.mass.edu/

Michigan
http://www.mde.state.mi.us/

Minnesota
http://www.educ.state.mn.us/

Mississippi
http://mdek12.state.ms.us/

Missouri
http://services.dese.state.mo.us/

Nebraska
http://www.nde.state.ne.us/

New Hampshire
http://www.state.nh.us/doe/education.html

New Jersey
http://www.state.nj.us/education/

New Mexico
http://www.nmche.org/

New York
http://www.nysed.gov/

North Dakota
http://www.sendit.nodak.edu/dpi/

Ohio
http://www.ode.ohio.gov/

Oklahoma
http://www.osrhe.edu/

Pennsylvania
http://www.state.pa.us/

Rhode Island
http://www.ri.net/RIDE/

South Dakota
http://www.state.sd.us/state/executive/deca/

Tennessee
http://www.state.tn.us/other/sde/homepage.htm

Texas
http://www.tenet.edu/

Utah
http://www.usoe.k12.ut.us/

Vermont
http://www.state.vt.us/educ.htm

Virginia
http://pen.k12.va.us/Anthology/VDOE/

Washington
http://www.ospi.wednet.edu/

West Virginia
http://access.k12.wv.us/

Wisconsin
http://www.state.wi.us/agencies/dpi/

If you want to discover what is going on in Canadian schools, an excellent gateway site can be found at:

Canada's "Master" Site for K-12
http://www.schoolnet.ca

Many corporate sites provide invaluable resources for teachers. For example, Apple Computer provides an outstanding site with information on hardware, software and activities such as building web sites and creating desktop movies.

Apple Computer's Education Site
http://www.apple.com/education/

Similar sites for the IBM corporation and Microsoft can be found at:

IBM's Education Site
http://www.solutions.ibm.com/k12

Microsoft's Education Site
http://www.microsoft.com/education/

Teachers can also use the Internet and the World Wide Web to explore specialized topics such as diversity and multiculturalism or more technically related areas such as learning disabilities or adaptive technology (using computers and related technologies to help children realize their full educational potential).

Diversity
http://www.execpc.com/~dboals/diversit.html

Inclusion Resources
http://www.hood.edu/seri/serihome.htm#inclusion_resources

Walk a Mile in My Shoes
http://www.wmht.org/trail/explor02.htm

Multicultural Pavilion
http://curry.edschool.Virginia.EDU/go/multicultural

Groups such as the Getty Information Institute are providing resources for teachers and scholars to connect to the arts and humanities, as well as to better understand how these areas are being redefined in a digital context.

Getty Information Institute
http://www.gii.getty.edu/giibroch/index.html

These are just a few examples of the types of resources that are available to teachers using the Internet and the World Wide Web. Like Esther Dyson, the computer and business guru, I am convinced that the Internet and the World Wide Web are profoundly redefining traditional institutions such as schools and universities. I believe, as she does, that the Internet and the World Wide Web give awesome power to individuals—the ability to be heard across the world, the ability to find information about almost everything" (Dyson, p. 7). And like Dyson, I recognize the potential to use this remarkable technology to spread lies, to commit fraud, and to harass people.

In the pages that follow I will try to provide educators with a basic and, I hope, useful introduction to using the Internet and the World Wide Web in their educational studies and then with suggestions on how to integrate them into their work as teachers in the classroom. In doing so, I want to emphasize that we are at a very important turning point in the history of education, schooling and teaching. Unlike critics such as Larry Cuban, I am convinced that the Internet and the World Wide Web are not passing educational technologies or fads but instead will profoundly redefine traditional modes of teaching and instruction. We need to provide our teachers with a useful introduction to this technology. That is the purpose of this book.

Chapter Two

The Internet and the World Wide Web

If you turn on the television news or pick up a popular magazine, it is probably hard not to come across some mention of the Internet and the World Wide Web. Fifteen years ago, the only people who would have known what the "Internet" meant were researchers in universities and the government. The World Wide Web did not even exist a decade ago. What is this remarkable technology? Where did it come from, and why is it so important?

What Is the Internet?

The Internet is a collection of millions of linked computers. It is hundreds of millions of people exchanging information and ideas. For teachers, it is a place where they can exchange lesson plans, check out curriculum standards in their field, chat with teachers who have interests similar to their own, find information for their classes, and have their students e-mail and correspond with other children from around the world.

For college students studying education, the Internet can be a tool to help you research information for almost any of your classes, keep in touch with your friends, and even present your work as a professional. Ultimately, the Internet is a tool to help you in your work as a teacher—a tool that, as this book will demonstrate, has extraordinary possibilities.

Technically, the Internet is a networked system of computers linked through high-speed connections. Its origins go back to the Cold War and the American military. In the early 1960s computer scientists and engineers working for the American military argued that it would be possible to connect computers with one another from different locations. These computers would be able to exchange information with one another using a common set of procedures.

In 1969, an experimental system known as ARPANET was used to connect computers at several American universities. In 1972 electronic or e-mail programs were sent for the first time. In the mid-1980s, the National Science Foundation set up five super-computing centers to provide high-speed access across the country. Helpful guides for becoming familiar with the Internet include:

EFF's [Extended] Guide to the Internet
http://www.cosy.sbg.ac.at/doc/eegtti

Learn the Internet
http://www.learnthenet.com/english/index.html

A comprehensive list of Internet guides and tutorials can be found at the following Library of Congress site.

Internet Guides, Tutorials, and Training Information Compiled by the Library of Congress
http://lcweb.loc.gov/global/internet/training.html

How Large Is the Internet?

The number of people on the Internet is very difficult to accurately determine. Current estimates (late 2000) are that there are 189.6 million English-speaking people using the Internet and 192.4 million non-English speaking users. These figures represent a total of 369.4 million users worldwide.

Internet statistics are changing so rapidly that the only way to keep up to date on the numbers is to visit organizations and their web sites compiling Internet usage information. In the United States, approximately 60% of American homes are connected to the Internet. Good sites to visit for current Internet use include:

Global Reach
http://www.glreach.com/globstats/index.php3

Internet States
http://www.internetstats.com/

What Is the World Wide Web?

A simple description of the World Wide Web is that it is a computer browsing system that makes it possible to navigate the Internet by pointing and clicking your computer mouse. The Web connects diverse sites by the use of hyperlinks, which are highlighted graphics such as a button, illustration, or piece of text that connects a user to another web site, source of information, or file on the Internet.

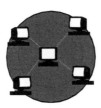

The World Wide Web is important because it has made the Internet accessible to the masses. Prior to the introduction of the World Wide Web, the use of the Internet was a much more difficult and largely text-based process. The individual responsible for creating the World Wide Web was Tim Berners-Lee, who was working at the European Particle Physics Laboratory (CERN) in Switzerland. Berners-Lee was interested in developing a computer-based communications system that would make it easier for scientists to communicate with one another. In December 1990 he wrote the first Web software and put it on the Internet the following summer.

Tim Berners-Lee Biography
http://www.w3.org/People/Berners-Lee/

For an interview with Tim Berners-Lee go to:

Interview with Tim Berners-Lee
http://www.ora.com/www/info/wj/issue3/tbl-int.html

Berners-Lee currently heads up the W3C (World Wide Web Consortium) organization, which is concerned with setting up standards for the World Wide Web. You can visit the Consortium at:

World Wide Web Consortium
http://www.w3.org

For background on the early history of the web and the role of Berners-Lee and CERN in its creation see:

An Overview of the Worldwide Web
http://public.web.cern.ch/Public/ACHIEVEMENTS/WEB/Welcome.html

The Web has been so successful in large part because it is based on open standards and protocols, including SGML (Standard Generalized Markup Language) and HTTP (Hypertext Transfer Protocol). HTML (Hypertext Markup Language), which is the language of the Web, is a subset of SGML.

Users of the Web do not need to know much about the standards and protocols that allow it to work. Knowing a little bit is helpful, though. For example, HTTP is the protocol that defines how requests for information and documents are transferred between clients and servers. You have probably noticed that the letters "http" are included at the beginning of most Web addresses. This is because the address indicates that it is using the Hypertext Transfer Protocol.

HTML is a special "language" that allows a document to be manipulated. There are commands in HTML, for example, for inserting certain sizes of texts, colored backgrounds, and the like. Once again, most users and even, as we will see later in this book, web creators don't need to know much about HTML, since web pages can be created by using a wide array of web editors. These web editors combine different functions to give them the feel of a traditional word processor or drawing program, but in fact they actually generate HTML code, which is what creates the web site.

Documents programmed in HTML can include traditional text sources or even drawings, photographs, sound files, and video. Web browsers interpret HTML tags that then display information in a relatively uniform format. Every web page is created using Hypertext Markup Language (HTML). You can view this code by clicking on the *Page Source* under the category in a browser like *Netscape Communicator*. Beneath the illustration of the home page from the American Memory Project that follows is the HTML code that it is based on.

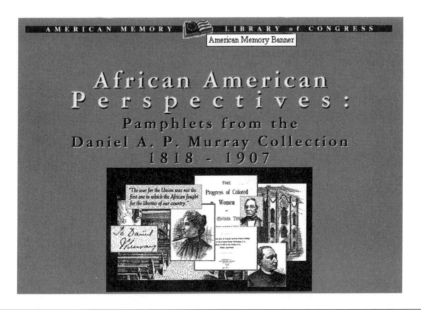

HTML Code for the Above Web Page "African American Perspectives" from the American Memory Project, Library of Congress

```
<body background="aapback.gif" bgcolor="#D6D6B5" link="#940818"
text="#100808" vlink="#420039">
<center><a href= "/ammem/ammemhome.html"><img src=
"/ammem/ammemicon3.gif
" alt="American Memory Banner" border=0></a></center>
<br><br>
<center><img src="afric_ban.gif" alt= "African-American Pamphlets from the
Daniel A. P. Murray Collection, 1880-1920"><br>
<img src= "afric_img.gif" alt="Collage"><br><br>
```

Hypertext Markup Language is important because it makes it possible to send information across the Internet in such a way that it can be read by different types of machines with different types of software. HTML documents often contain hypertext links, which, when clicked, take the user to another document or object. These links are one of the most interesting aspects of the Web. They make it possible for the millions of different documents that reside on the World Wide Web to be interconnected.

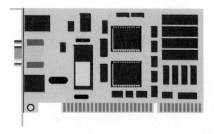

Tim Berners-Lee describes how he initially thought of the World Wide Web: "as a universal space in which all information could be put to get over the tremendous problems of incompatibility between servers, different data formats and different interactive databases such as VAX Notes and Usenet news. I was interested in it being very much of a space in which it was easy to add information.... The idea was that putting stuff on the Web should be trivial just like reading it and with the original World Wide Web program it was. You could make a link just by hitting a key. As you browsed, you could have many documents open at once" (Kirsner, 1996).

How Do I Connect to the Internet?

In order to connect to the Internet and the World Wide Web, you will need a computer with a communications program or "browser." If you are off campus, you can connect your computer to the Internet through a modem. On campus in a lab or in a dormitory you are most likely going to be able to connect into a local network, which will then connect you to the Internet. If you use a regular telephone line to connect your computer to the Internet, you need to remember that while you are connected the line cannot be used for regular calls.

If you are connecting to the Internet and the World Wide Web off campus, you almost certainly will be doing so with a modem. A modem is a device that allows you to connect your computer to a telephone and to send messages via a telephone line. It can be internal and housed within your computer, or it can be external and sit outside of your computer. Modems convert digital signals from the computer (0s and 1s) to audio signals. This process allows you to use your telephone line in order to establish a communications link.

Modem speeds are measured in bits per second (bps). This is what is called a baud rate. A couple of years ago, standard modem speeds were 2400 bps. Now they run anywhere from 28,800 bps to 56,800 bps and are getting faster all of the time.

Cable modems are becoming widespread in many homes. These provide download speeds enormously faster than telephone-connected systems, making it practical to transmit multimedia files such as movies on the Internet. Using a 28.8 bps telephone modem, a 2MB file can be downloaded in 9.3 minutes. Using a 56.8 bps this same file would take 4.65 minutes to download. With a cable modem it would take 10 seconds.

Cable modems transmit over digital fiber optic cable. They do not require an extra telephone line. For more information about cable modems consult the following sites:

Cable Modems Frequently Asked Questions
http://www.cox.com/CoxatHome/faq.asp

Generally speaking, you want to get the fastest modem possible, because this will determine how fast information can be received. This becomes even more important when you are receiving information with extensive graphic and sound files. Text-based files transfer very quickly.

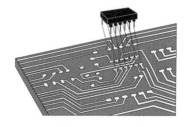

If you connect off campus through a commercial network, it will cost you between $15 to $20 a month. This service will typically allow you to connect for 40 to 50 hours. For a small additional fee you can get unlimited access with most services. Find out if there is a discount provided through your school or if you can dial into your school's network for free.

In order to access your university network or a commercial network, you will have to use a password. Using a password keeps other people from using your account. You should not share your password with others. Think of it as being like the keys to your car. You don't give them out to just anyone. Make sure that you remember your password so that you can get access to your account. Use the name of a favorite pet or a character you like from a book or movie.

If you have further questions about the Internet and the World Wide Web you may find the following web sites helpful.

Internet FAQ Archives
http://www.faqs.org/faqs/top.html

World Wide Web FAQs
http://www.boutell.com/faq

World Wide Web Frequently Asked Questions
http://humanities.uchicago.edu/homes/mark/WWW_FAQ.html

Chapter Three

Internet and Web Basics

There are certain things you need to know in order to use the Internet and the World Wide Web. These include understanding how computer networks like the Internet operate, what web browsers are and how they work, how to search for information using a web browser, the fundamentals of e-mail, and so on. In the following chapter an introduction to these basics is provided.

What Is a Computer Network?

The Internet and the World Wide Web are based around the idea of networking. Essentially a network connects one computer to another so that they can exchange information and communicate with each other. Networks can be almost any size. Two computers connected together by a wire (a null modem) and a file transfer program are a network. The Internet, which may have as many as 30 million computers connected to it, is also a network. Think of it as a giant spider web with the separate strands connecting together its different parts.

Not all computer networks are part of the Internet. Many networks stand by themselves. Many of them connect to the Internet, so the user does not realize that they are moving off a local network onto a larger system—similar to moving from a local street onto a superhighway.

There are, for example, commercial networks such as CompuServe, Microsoft Network, and America Online that charge user fees and provide a wide range of services including databases, electronic bulletin boards, and discussion groups. CompuServe, for example, was begun in 1969 and serves 4.5 million customers. It includes special features such as an online encyclopedia, live chat channels, news and information from the Cable News Network, *Worlds Away* (a virtual world chat system in which the user can actually create a body [an avatar] who will navigate through the program), a shopping network, and an entertainment network for children.

CompuServe
http://www.compuserve.com

America Online (AOL) has services such as *ABC Sports Online*, an hourly summary of news from Reuters news service, travel and shopping services from American Express, and reference sources such as *Grolier Multimedia Encyclopedia* and the *Merriam-Webster Collegiate Dictionary*.

America Online
http://www.aol.com

The Microsoft Network includes services such as an online version of the multimedia encyclopedia *Encarta*, travel guides, an online version of the newspaper *U.S.A. Today,* and a forum for using *Windows 95*.

The Microsoft Network
http://www.msn.com

There are nonprofit networks that are run by nonprofit organizations and are generally dedicated to issues such as education, the environment, or peace. Private networks can be set up by a private business or public institution. The consulting firm of Ernst & Young, for example, has an extensive private network that allows its employees to exchange information and to stay in contact with one another. Regional networks serve a particular region. Big Sky Telegraph in Montana, for example, is a network that serves people living in the West and allows them to exchange information and resources.

Big Sky Telegraph
http://macsky.bigsky.dillon.mt.us/

Finally, there are state networks that operate in almost every state in the country. In Florida, the FIRN system provides a statewide educational networking system for teachers in the K–12 and university systems. It is paid for from taxes and is provided to its users for free.

FIRN
http://www.firn.edu/about.html

What Is a Web Browser?

A web browser is a type of software that provides users with a graphical interface for connecting to and navigating through the World Wide Web. By clicking on different items on the computer screen (hyperlinks, scroll bars, and so on) the user is able to connect to different web sites and navigate through the information that is included on them.

Web browsers have evolved rapidly in recent years. Older programs such as Lynx are text based. If you are using an older and less powerful computer, or your university has not updated its systems, you may find yourself having to use a text-based browser. This will be unfortunate, because one of the most interesting features of the World Wide Web is its visual and graphic capability. Sophisticated graphics and multimedia materials can be accessed using Microsoft's *Internet Explorer* and Netscape's *Navigator*.

Internet Explorer and *Navigator* are the two most popular browser programs currently in use. Microsoft and Netscape are in fierce competition with each other to dominate the browser market. At the present time, Netscape is still the most widely used browser. Microsoft, however, is gradually gaining ground.

In general, Explorer and Navigator work approximately the same way. Some terminology is different, and both are being constantly upgraded to make them more competitive with one another. It seems as though an upgraded version of each product is available once or twice a year.
Both products can be loaded free off of the Internet. I would suggest that you get used to using both products and find out which suits you best. You can connect to download sites for both companies by visiting the two following addresses:

Microsoft Internet Explorer
http://www.microsoft.com/windows/ie/default.htm

Netscape Navigator
http://home.netscape.com

Although Netscape and Microsoft dominate the web browser business, there are many other web browsers available. You may want to explore the following sites to learn more about these other systems.

NCSA Mosaic
http://www.ncsa.uiuc.edu/SDG/Software/Mosaic/

NetCruiser
http://www.netcom.com/software

Opera 2.12
http://opera.nta.no

Web Browsers and How They Work

At this time, *Microsoft Explorer* and *Netscape Communicator* are the most widely used browsers in the world. Both function in similar ways. Because you can download them free from the Internet, there is no reason not to have both programs on your computer.

Trying to describe in detail all of the functions of a web browser is a bit like trying to teach someone how to drive a car by giving him or her printed instructions. You need to use a web browser to get a clear sense of what it will actually do. Find a friend who has experience going online and ask him or her to show you the basics. Remember that there are extensive *help* functions built into both browsers.

The following brief "Anatomy of a Web Browser" should help you get a general sense of a typical web browser's main functions.

Anatomy of a Web Browser

Shown below are the main features for the browser Netscape Communicator. A very similar interface can be found on Microsoft's Netscape Explorer browser. These two browsers represent over 95 percent of the current browser market.

Bookmark allows you to record the address of the web site you are visiting without having to type it and so you can visit it easily again.

              Address will connect like a telephone number to the web site.

Back shows the last web page you viewed.

       Forward will take you back to the page or pages you first viewed.

       Reload refreshes the web page you are looking at.

       Home returns you to your home page.

       Search connects you to a search engine or directory.

       Guide connects you to a guide for the browser.

       Print lets you print the file you are looking at.

       Security shows security information for your computer.

       Stop interrupts the transfer of data from the Internet to your computer.

The Anatomy of a Web Address

A web address is a little bit like a telephone number. Each address is unique, but it also has a very specific logic—going from the general at the beginning to the more specific at the end. Look at the following address for the White House in Washington, DC. The address is technically referred to as a Universal Resource Locator (URL). Here are what its different parts mean.

White House
http://www.whitehouse.gov

http:// is an abbreviation for Hypertext Transport Protocol. When a colon follows http with two forward slashes it indicates that you are connecting to a web document rather than some other type of Internet site such as a File Transfer Protocol (FTP) site or a Gopher.

www. tells you that what follows is the name of the web server where the web site for this address can be found.

.whitehouse tells you the name of the organization where the web page is located.

.gov is the final suffix and is known as a zone name. Different zone names indicate different types of web sites: **.org**, for example, generally indicates a nonprofit organization, while **.com** indicates a commercial web site and **.edu** an educational site.

In order to use an address to visit a site, type it into the address window, and click it with your mouse or hit "enter." The browser will then connect your computer with the site.

How Is Information Actually Transferred?

What actually happens when you connect to a web site through your browser? Let's assume that you are making a connection through an Internet provider from your home. The following takes place:

1. Connected to the Internet, you type a web address into your browser. Let's use the White House address again:

White House
http://www.whitehouse.gov

2. Software on your computer breaks your message—the command to go to a specific web site address—into a *packet,* which is then forwarded to your modem. If you are transferring large amounts of information (a lengthy report, multiple graphic files, and so on) the packets you send may travel different routes on the Internet before they are joined together at their final destination.

3. Your modem converts the data in the address from a binary to an analog signal. This allows the information to be communicated over telephone lines.

4. Your message is sent to your Internet provider.

5. Your Internet provider sends your message to a routing computer at another site.

6. Your message is processed at the router site and then sent out to the web site that you are trying to visit.

7. You connect with the White House web site at:

The White House
http://www.whitehouse.gov

Information from the web site you have contacted (The White House) is sent back by reversing the process.

Search Engines and Directories

There are two main ways to search for information using the World Wide Web. The first is a search engine. In order to get to a search engine open up your web browser and click on **search.** When the search engine is linked to your computer, you can type in the subject you are looking for. To activate the search you need to hit **submit** or **enter**.

Search engines look for information based on Boolean Logic. Boolean Logic is named after the nineteenth century English mathematician George Boole. Boolean logic or algebra has to do with logical or true/false values. Variables in Boolean algebra can be limited by operators such as "and," "or," and "not.[EFP, Jr.1]"

Search operators are often different among various search engines. You will have to check the Help file in your search engine to make sure what operators are actually in use. Some widely used operators include:

" " **Quotation marks** Combine all of the information in a phrase or sentence.

and Combines or links together key words. A + sign can often be used in place of **and**.

Or Searches using a specific criteria when there are two or more search terms.

Near Placed between two search terms to locate information that may be near each other in a document ("zoos" and "lions," for example).

* Asterisk. Used to connect sources that are spelled in related ways. (**Saint***, for example, will generate links to words as different as "Saint Thomas" and "Saint Louis").

But not Includes certain specific criteria, but not others ("baseball players," **but not** "Babe Ruth").

An example of using Boolean logic to conduct a search on Brenda Laurel—a leading computer theorist and video game developer— and her interest in video games and gender discrimination might look something like this:

"Laurel, Brenda **and** video games **or** computer games **and** gender **and** equity."

Some of the most popular search engines for the World Wide Web include:

Alta Vista
http://altavista.digital.com

Excite
http://excite.com

Infoseek
http://guide.infoseek.com

Webcrawler
http://www.webcrawler.com

Web directories are different than search engines. Basically, web directories are detailed lists of topics on a particular subject. Some of the most popular web directories include:

Galaxy
http://galaxy.einet.net

Magellan
http://magellan.mckinley.com

Yahoo
http://www.yahoo.com

The Yellow Pages
http://theyellowpages.com

Try many different search engines and directories to see the ones that work best for you. The author, for example, finds that Infoseek and Yahoo are particularly effective for him. Note how different search engines and directories will provide you with different results. A solution to this problem is to try a meta engine or directory, which combines different search engines and directories together.

Google
http://www.google.com/

Metacrawler
http://www.metacrawler.com

Prime Search
http://www.delta.com/prime.com/pssearch.htm

All-in-one search pages can be found at:

All-In-One-Search Page
http://www.allonesearch.com/

The Argus Clearing House
http://www.clearinghouse.net/

Galaxy
http://galaxy.tradewave.com/

Microsoft
http://www.msn.com.access/allonone.asp

Netscape
http://www.netscape.com/home/internet-search.html

Savy Search
http://www.search.com/

Reviews and comparisons of search engines can be found at:

A Guide to Web Directories
http://www.crosswinds.net/~directories/home.htm

Understanding and Comparing Web Research Tools
http://www.hamline.edu/administration/libraries/search/comparisons.html

Search Engine Showdown
http://www.searchengineshowdown.com/

Search Engine Watch
http://searchenginewatch.com/

Using Bookmarks

Typing in an e-mail address can be very tedious. If you revisit a site, particularly on a regular basis, you don't want to have to retype it. Also, if you like a site and want to revisit it, you will want to be able to remember the address. Bookmarks are the solution to both of these problems.

In Netscape Navigator you can organize bookmarks and edit them by clicking on **Bookmarks** from the Windows menu. By clicking on the **Add Bookmark** command, you can add any web site you are visiting as a bookmark. In Microsoft Explorer you can organize web addresses by clicking on **Favorites.**

As you develop large collections of web addresses, you will want to organize them in different categories. You can do this by creating folders for them. To learn more about this process consult the help file in your browser for bookmarks.

What is E-Mail?

E-mail is one of the most useful Internet tools for college students. Most universities and colleges now provide e-mail addresses for students throughout their course of study. Get your e-mail address as soon as you start your studies, and you can use it for staying in touch with friends and relatives, reaching out to other students around the country, participating in discussion groups of interest to you, and communicating with other students on your campus, as well as with the professors for your courses.

Technically, e-mail stands for electronic mail. It is a messaging system that allows Internet users to send messages back and forth much like the postal system. Most e-mail is text-based, although it is increasingly including graphics, sound, and even video.

E-mail is cool for lots of reasons. To begin with, it doesn't require stamps and envelopes or going to the post office to send something. E-mail can be sent and received any time of the day or night. It is instantaneous. Documents, a term paper, or a long project proposal can be sent along with e-mail messages as attachments.

The disadvantages of e-mail are that you need a computer to send it, and not everyone has access either to a computer with an Internet connection or an e-mail address of his or her own. Just as when you log onto the Internet, you will have to use a password to connect to your e-mail. Follow the same security procedures to keep your mail private.

Anatomy of an E-Mail Address

E-mail addresses are similar to web addresses. Each e-mail address is unique. It also has a very specific logic—like a web address going from the general at the beginning of an address to the more specific at the end. Look at the following e-mail address for the President of the United States at the White House in Washington, DC.

White House Address for the President
president@whitehouse.gov

User Name In this case, *president.* Names cannot be used more than once for any subscriber on a system. With common names like Smith, this could present a problem, but having numbers follow the name solves it.

@ The "at" sign literally tells you the service provider who supports the e-mail address.

whitehouse Tells you the name of the provider for the e-mail address.

. The period separates the various domains of the address.

gov Indicates the type of organization that the provider is, in this case, a government organization.

If you are interested in looking up e-mail addresses for friends or famous people, there are several groups that run web sites that will help you. These include:

FAQ: How to Find People's E-Mail Addresses
http://www.qucis.queensu.ca/FAQs/email/finding.html

Getting Connected for E- Mail

To get connected and use e-mail at home or off campus, you will need a computer with a modem, communications software, and a telephone connection to an Internet service provider, specialty mail service, or an online service like America Online. If you are connecting through a student mail service at your university or college, there will almost certainly be a set of forms you will need to complete to be able to establish your own e-mail address and to begin to send and receive messages.

The major web browsers have e-mail functions built into them. You may want to use a specialized e-mail program like Eudora.

Eudora
http://www.access-us.com/eud5.htm

E-mail mechanically works in much the same way as the World Wide Web. Once you have typed your letter on an e-mail program, it is encoded by a modem and converted to an analog message. Then it is sent to your service provider where it is sent out on the Internet to the recipient's provider and put in his or her mailbox. Once the message is received it waits for the addressee who can request that it be downloaded from the Internet provider.

To learn more about sending e-mail messages, visit the following sites:

A Beginner's Guide to Effective E-mail:
http://www.webfoot.com/advice/email.top.html

You can learn how e-mail can be used with students in the classroom:

Intercultural E-mail Classroom Connections
http://www.stolaf.edu/network/iecc

If, for fun, you want to send e-mail messages with pictures, take a look at the following web site sponsored by MIT.

The Electric Postcard
http://postcards.www.media.mit.edu/Postcards

Discussion Lists and Chat Rooms

Discussion lists and servers are Internet programs that make it possible for persons with interests in the same subject to connect with one another and exchange ideas. Discussion lists have the advantage of bringing together people from different places at different times and lets them freely exchange ideas and information. The author, for example, is currently part of a discussion group at the University of Miami that is considering how to update the school's library and its facilities. The discussion list that has been set up includes librarians, staff, faculty, and students. Postings are left for the discussion group by people at times that suit them. A permanent trail or archive of the emerging discussion is left for reference. A list of web-based discussion groups and information about how to sign up for them can be found at:

Deja News
http://www.deja.com/usenet

Liszt
http://www.liszt.com/

Search the List of Lists
http://catalog.com/vivian/interest-group-search.html

Chat rooms are electronic discussion programs that make it possible for people to interact with each other in real time—i.e., exchange messages with each other live. Chat rooms are particularly popular with network providers like America Online.

Netiquette

Whether you are using e-mail or going online in a discussion group or chat room, there are rules of appropriate behavior that need to be followed. These rules are commonly referred to as "netiquette."

As a general rule, treat others the same way that you would like to be treated yourself. Avoid abusive and foul language. Do not interfere with another person's mail files or postings. **DO NOT TYPE IN ALL CAPS OR IN BOLD!** It is considered rude and the same as shouting in a conversation. Do not fill people's mailboxes with all sorts of irrelevant postings. This is known as "spamming." Because you wrote something doesn't mean everybody needs to read it.

E-Mail Etiquette
http://www.iwillfollow.com/email.htm

Netiquette Homepage by Arlene H. Rinaldi
http://www.fau.edu/rinaldi/net

Netiquette mostly involves using common sense online. Nobody wants to put up with a fool or look like one to other people.

Chapter Four

The Internet as a Tool for Your Studies in Education

The Internet and the World Wide Web are ideal resources for people interested in studying education and teaching. The federal government provides rich sources of information on many of its web sites for educators. Often they will even provide answers to specific questions. AskERIC, for example, is a site funded by the United States Department of Education that will provide you e-mail answers to questions you have about education.

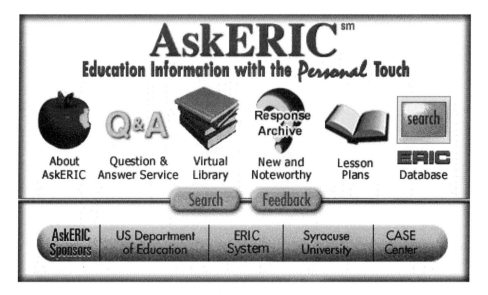

AskERIC Virtual Library
http://ericir.syr.edu/

Probably the best place to begin to search on your own for information on education is the U.S. Department of Education. The various web sites of this federal office include extensive statistical data as well as reports by researchers and government officials. Suppose, for example, you have an assignment to write an essay on the conditions of schools in the United States or on the work of teachers. At the U.S. Department of Education web site you can find the information, key references and links to sources that will help you complete your assignment.

U.S. Department of Education
http://www.ed.gov

Additional government web sites concerned with education can be searched for at:

Government Web Sites
http://www.ipcress.com/writer/gov.html

Many web sites are not specifically focused on education as a subject but have information and resources that deal directly with educational issues. Say, for example, that you are interested in learning about Supreme Court Cases that have affected American education such as the 1954 Brown v. Topeka desegregation case. The following web sites could prove invaluable:

Oyez Oyez Oyez
http://oyez.at.nwu.edu/oyez.html

Supreme Court Decisions
http://www.law.cornell.edu/supct/supct.table.html

Information about nonpublic and alternative education is also available on the World Wide Web. Homeschooling, for example, where parents educate their children themselves, is an increasingly popular movement. Resources on this topic can be found at:

Homeschooling Information
http://www.home-ed-press.com

There are many different web sites that will provide you with background and information on national curriculum standards and requirements. A good site on educational standards with excellent links is the Putnam Valley, New York, school district's site:

Developing Educational Standards
http://putwest.boces.org/Standards.html

Examples of specialized web sites dealing with national curriculum standards include:

National Standards for United States History
http://www.sscnet.ucla.edu/nchs/us-toc.htm

Eisenhower National Clearinghouse: Standards and Frameworks
http://www.enc.org/professional/standards/

Project 206: Science Literacy for a Changing Future
http://project2061.aaas.org/

If you are interested in different types of information about colleges and universities, the following web sites will be of interest.

American University Links
http://www.clas.ufl.edu/CLAS/american-universities.html

Black Colleges and Universities
http://www.edonline.com/cq/hbcu

Peterson's Education Center
http://www.petersons.com/ugrad

U.S. News College Center
http://www.usnews.com/usnews/edu/?/home.html

Introduction to Education

The web is an ideal place to learn about schools and teaching. Among the best starting points to research about accreditation issues and requirements for entering the profession is the National Council for the Accreditation of Teacher Education (NCATE).

National Council for the Accreditation of Teacher Education
http://www.ncate.org/

You can connect to other teachers for help on lesson plans, professional planning, and similar types of issues by connecting to Teacher Talk at Indiana University:

Teacher Talk
http://www.pacificnet.net/~mandel//index.html

Teachers Helping Teachers describes itself as a service that provides "basic teaching tips to inexperienced teachers; ideas that can be immediately implemented into the classroom... new ideas in teaching methodologies for all teachers... (and) a forum for experienced teachers to share their expertise and tips with colleagues around the world."

Teachers Helping Teachers
http://education.indiana.edu/cas/tt/tthmpg.html

The rest of this chapter provides an introduction to some of the many web sites that can be used to study various topics in education. Many of these web sites can be used across different areas. Think of this list as a starting point. You can continue to add to and build on it as you become more familiar with different types of resources on the Internet.

Social and Cultural Foundations

For national attitudes and opinions dealing with not only schools, but American society in general, visit the Gallup Organization:

Gallup Organization
http://www.gallup.com/

Information on Civil Rights and equity issues can be found at:

Museum of Tolerance
http://www.wiesenthal.com/mot

National Civil Rights Museum
http://www.midsouth.rr.com/civilrights/

An excellent set of links for different aspects of the Afro-American experience can be found at:

The Universal Black Pages
http://www.ubp.com/

Links on Chicano and Latino culture can be found at:

Chicano/Latino Net
http://latino.sscnet.ucla.edu/

Native American links are available at:

Native Web
http://www.nativeweb.org/

For general sources on diversity and education visit:

University of Maryland Diversity Database
http://www.inform.umd.edu/EdRes/Topic/Diversity/

Excellent materials on gender equity can be found at:

The American Association of University Women
http://www.aauw.org/index.html

Make sure to connect to the following page at the American Association of University Women for educational equity materials:

Research on Gender Equity
http://www.aauw.org/2000/research.html

Other gender equity resources can be found at:

Equity Online
http://www.edc.org/WomensEquity/

Use the following site to learn about population trends (how many people teach, who goes to school, and the like). You can even find census data for the community you live in.

U.S. Census Bureau
http://www.census.gov

The U.S. Department of Education includes extensive research reports and compilations of data for many topics you may need to explore in the social foundations area. Who are dropouts? What are the employment projections for teachers? What is the representation of different racial and minority groups in the public schools? How many private school students are there in the United States? These are just a few examples of the type of information that is available.

U.S. Department of Education
http://www.ed.gov/

Psychological Foundations

Many of the web-based resources that you are most likely to be interested in for the field of educational psychology will be found at psychology web sites such as:

Brown University, Department of Cognitive and Linguistic Sciences
http://www.cog.brown.edu/index.html

Individual figures important in educational psychology and psychology can also be researched. For example, background on the Swiss psychologist Jean Piaget is available at:

The Jean Piaget Society
http://www.piaget.org/

To learn about the Russian constructivist Lev Vygotsky, you can visit:

Lev Semenovich Vygotsky
http://www.massey.ac.nz/~ALock/virtual/project2.htm

School psychology resources can be found online at:

School Psychology Resources Online
http://mail.bcpl.lib.md.us/~sandyste/school_psych.html

Special Education

The Web provides exceptional resources for those interested in different areas of special education. Separate sites can be found for various areas of special needs, as well as on the use of computers by individuals with special needs.

Apple's The Disability Connection
http://www2.apple.com/disability/disability_home.html

Autism Resources
http://web.syr.edu/~jmwobus/autism/

Blind Links
http://www.seidata.com/~marriage/rblind.html

Deaf World Web
http://deafworldweb.org/dww

Down Syndrome
http://www.nas.com/downsyn/index.html

Council for Exceptional Children
http://www.cec.sped.org/

Eric Clearinghouse on Disabilities and Gifted Education
http://ericec.org/index.html

Family Village
http://www.familyvillage.wisc.edu/

National Information Center for Children and Youths with Disabilities
http://www.nichcy.org/

Learning Disabilities Association of America
http://205.164.116.200/LDA/index.html

Office of Special Education Programs
http://www.ed.gov/offices/OSERS/OSEP/index.html

Scotter's Low Vision Land
http://www.community.net/~byndsght/welcome.html

Society for the Autistically Handicapped
http://giraffe.rmplc.co.uk/eduweb/sites/autism

Special Education Links
http://www.mts.net/~jgreenco/special.html

Special Education Resources on the Internet
http://www.hood.edu/seri/serihome.htm

Special Education Resources, University of Virginia
http://curry.edschool.virginia.edu/go/specialed/

Gifted Education

Like the more general field of special education, gifted education is well represented on the Internet.

Center for Talent Development
http://www.yahoo.com/education/k_12/gifted_youth/

Gifted and Talented Education
http://www.egusd.k12.ca.us/webdocs/gate.html

Johns Hopkins University, Center for Talented Youth (CTY)
Gopher://juniverse.hcf.jhu.edu:10005/11/.gifted

National Association of Gifted Education
http://www.nagc.org/

Stanford Education Program for Gifted Youth (EPGY)
http://kanpai.stanford.edu/epgy/pamoh/pamoh.html

Multicultural Education

Multicultural education sources on the Internet and World Wide Web include a wide range of resources, from information on historical figures like Martin Luther King to sources on Native American people. A good place to begin to link to different curriculum resources is the web site "Walk a Mile in My Shoes:"

Walk a Mile in My Shoes: Multicultural Curriculum Resources
http://www.wmht.org/trail/explor02.htm

Other useful sites are the University of Virginia School of Education's
Multicultural Pavilion and the diversity site at :

Multicultural Pavilion
http://curry.edschool.Virginia.EDU/go/multicultural/

CLNET
http://clnet.ucr.edu/

If you want to explore books on multicultural topics, connect to:

Multicultural Book Review Homepage
http://w.isomedia.com/homes/jmele/homepage.html

Interesting Native American sites can be found at:

The Indian Pueblo Cultural Center
http://hanksville.phast.umass.edu/defs/independent/PCC/PCC.html#toc

Index of Native American Source on the Internet
http://hanksville.phast.umass.edu:80/misc/NAresources.html

Maya/Aztec/Inca Center
http://www.realtime.net/maya/

Migration and Ethnic Relations
http://www.ercomer.org/wwwvl/

Native American Indian Resources
http://indy4.fdl.cc.mn.us/~isk/mainmenu.html

Computers and Education

Technology Education Home Page
http://ed1.eng.ohio-state.edu/

WWW Virtual Library: Educational Technology
http://tecfa.unige.ch/info-edu-comp.html

Information about Internet filters and protecting children can be found at:

Internet Safety for Kids
http://www.ou.edu/oupd/kidsafe/warn_kid.htm

Tips for Safer Surfing
http://www.safesurf.com/lifegard.htm

Children's Literature and Language Arts

An excellent starting point for learning about children's literature on the web is:

Carol Hurst's Children's Literature Site
http://www.carolhurst.com/

The Children's Literature Web Guide
http://www.ucalgary.ca/~dkbrown/index.html

The WEB: Celebrating Children's Literature
http://www.armory.com/~web/web.html

You can go online to ask well-known children's authors questions by visiting the following site:

"Ask the Author"
http://ipl.sils.umich.edu/youth/AskAuthor/

Other web sites on children's literature, folklore, and mythology include:

Classics for Young People
http://www.ucalgary.ca/~dkbrown/storclas.html

Kindred Spirits (L. M. Mongomery Institute)
http://www.upei.ca/~lmmi/cover.html

Laura Ingalls Wilder Home Page
http://webpages.marshall.edu/~irby1/laura.htmlx

The Little Red Riding Hood Project
http://www-dept.usm.edu/~engdept/lrrh/lrrhhome.htm

Newbery Award Home Page
http://www.ala.org/alsc/newbery.html

The Grimm Brothers
http://www.who2.com/thebrothersgrimm.html

Cyber Seuss
http://www.afn.org/~afn15301/drseuss.html

Tales of Wonder: Folk and Fairy Tales from Around the World
http://www.ccsd.k12.wy.us/fourth/africa.html

Winnie the Pooh and Friends
http://worldkids.net/pooh/welcome.html

Mythology and Folklore

Encylopedia Mythica
http://www.pantheon.org/mythica/

Folklore, Myth and Legend
http://www.ucalgary.ca/~dkbrown/storfolk.html

Folklore and Mythology Electronic Texts
http://www.pitt.edu/~dash/folktexts.html

Mythology and Folklore
http://www.pibburns.com/mythfolk.htm

Mythology
http://www.pibburns.com/mythfolk.htm

Mermaids
http://www.mermaid.net/

Mythology in Western Art
http://www-lib.haifa.ac.il/www/art/mythology_westart.html

Social Studies Methods

Social Studies, because of its use of original documents (diaries, deeds, census records) and visual sources (photographs, art work, maps), is an extremely rich area on the Internet and the World Wide Web. Excellent gateway sites include:

The History Page
http://www.searchbeat.com/history.htm

World History Compass
http://www.worldhistorycompass.com/index.htm

If you want to find out what happened on a specific date visit This Day in History:

This Day in History
http://www.9online.com/today/today.htm

Individual historical periods can be found at sites such as:

Civil War
http://www.janke.washcoll.edu/civilwar/civilwar.htm

The Psychedelic '60s
http://www.lib.virginia.edu/exhibits/sixties/

General history and social studies web sites can be linked to at:

History in the Classroom
http://www.pbs.org/history/class.html

History/Social Studies Web Site for K–12 Teachers
http://www.execpc.com/~dboals/boals.html

Social Studies
http://www.csun.edu/~vceed009/socialstudies.html

Genealogy is a great subject to integrate into courses in American history, as well as state and local history. Gateway sites can be found at:

Genealogy.Com
http://genealogy.emcee.com/

Gengateway.Com
http://www.gengateway.com/

Gen Source (Genealogy Gateway)
http://www.gensource.com/ifoundit/

More practical "how to do it" sites can be found at:

Genealogy "How-To" Guide
http://www.familytreemaker.com/mainmenu.html

Family Search
http://www.familysearch.org/

The Genealogy Page (National Archives)
http://www.nara.gov/genealogy/

Surname Origin List
http://www.familychronicle.com/surname.htm

The art and architecture of cemeteries and tombstones is a fascinating topic. It can be explored at length by visiting:

Tombstone Rubbings
http://www.firstct.com/fv/t_stone.html

Maps are an invaluable resource for social studies teachers at all levels of the educational system. The World Wide Web has many excellent map resources. Among the most useful are:

Click a Map
http://www.atlapedia.com/online/map_index.htm

Earth Rise
http://earthrise.sdsc.edu/

Geography Resources from the U.S. Census Bureau
http://www.census.gov/geo/www/

How Far is It?
http://www.indo.com/distance/

Maps of the World
http://www.lib.utexas.edu/Libs/PCL/Map_collection/world_maps.html

Quick Maps
http://www.theodora.com/maps/abc_world_maps.html

U.S. Gazeteer (U.S. Census Bureau)
http://www.census.gov/cgi-bin/gazetteer/

Vintage Panoramic Maps (Library of Congress)
http://lcweb2.loc.gov/ammem/pmhtml/

A gateway for historical documents that can be used by teachers can be found at:

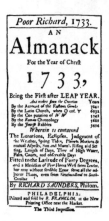

Historical Documents
http://w3.one.net/~mweiler/ushda/list.htm

Examples of sites with excellent collections of historical documents include:

Documents in Law, History and Diplomacy
http://www.yale.edu/lawweb/avalon/avalon.htm

Thomas Historical Documents
http://lcweb2.loc.gov/const/constquery.html

Emancipation Proclamation
http://www.nps.gov/ncro/anti/emancipation.html

Historical Documents
http://odur.let.rug.nl/~usa/D/

If you want to find different types of history timelines to use in your classes, then go to the following gateway site:

History Timelines
http://www.searchbeat.com/history.htm

If you find yourself teaching a course that includes information on your state or local community, you will find the following state addresses helpful:

Alabama
http://alaweb.asc.edu/

Alaska
http://www.state.ak.us/

Arizona
http://www.state.az.us/

Arkansas
http://www.state.ar.us/

California
http://www.ca.gov/

Colorado
http://www.state.co.us/

Delaware
http://www.state.de.us/

Florida
http://www.state.fl.us/gsd/

Georgia
http://www.state.ga.us/

Hawaii
http://www.state.hi.us/

Idaho
http://www.accessidaho.org/index.html

Illinois
http://www.state.il.us/

Indiana
http://www.state.in.us/

Iowa
http://www.state.ia.us/

Kansas
http://www.state.ks.us/

Kentucky
http://www.state.ky.us/

Louisiana
http://www.state.la.us/

Maine
http://www.state.me.us/

Maryland
http://www.mec.state.md.us/

Massachusetts
http://www.state.ma.us/

Michigan
http://www.migov.state.mi.us/

Minnesota
http://www.state.mn.us/

Mississippi
http://www.state.ms.us

Missouri
http://www.state.mo.us/

Nebraska
http://www.state.ne.us/

Nevada
http://www.state.nv.us/

New Hampshire
http://www.state.nh.us/

New Jersey
http://www.state.nj.us/

New Mexico
http://www.state.nm.us/

New York
http://www.state.ny.us/

North Carolina
http://www.state.nc.us/

North Dakota
http://www.state.nd.us/

Ohio
http://www.state.oh.us/

Oklahoma
http://www.state.ok.us/

Oregon
http://www.state.or.us/

Pennsylvania
http://www.state.pa.us/

Rhode Island
http://www.info.state.ri.us/

South Carolina
http://www.state.sc.us/

South Dakota
http://www.state.sd.us/

Tennessee
http://www.state.tn.us/

Texas
http://www.state.tx.us/

Utah
http://www.state.ut.us/

Vermont
http://www.cit.state.vt.us/

Virginia
http://www.state.va.us/

Washington
http://www.state.wa.us/

West Virginia
http://www.state.wv.us/

Wisconsin
http://www.state.wi.us/

Wyoming
http://www.state.wy.us/

Information on world cultures can be found at the following web addresses:

3-D Atlas Online
http://www.3datlas.com/

Asia Society
http://www.asiasociety.org/

Data Base Europe
http://www.asg.physik.uni-erlangen.de/europa/indexe.htm

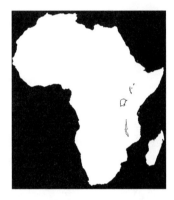

Index on Africa
http://www.africaindex.africainfo.no/

Latin American Information Network
http://www.lanic.utexas.edu/

The World Factbook
http://www.odci.gov/cia/publications/factbook/

Online sources related to Economics that could be useful in the classroom include:

Economic Statistics
http://www.cbs.nl/en/services/links/default.asp

History of Economic Thought
http://socserv2.socsci.mcmaster.ca/~econ/ugcm/3ll3/

If you want to explore inflation and the consumer price index visit:

Federal Reserve System
http://www.federalreserve.gov/

Consumer Price Indexes
http://stats.bls.gov/cpihome.htm

Inflation Calculators
http://www.jsc.nasa.gov/bu2/inflate.html

Gateway sites for Archeology include:

Archeology Related Links
http://www.arch.dcr.state.nc.us/links.htm

Arch Net
http://archnet.uconn.edu/

Examples of Archeological sites that can be used to support teaching include:

Biblical Archeology
http://www.lpl.arizona.edu/~kmeyers/archaeol/bib_arch.html

Classics and Mediterranean Archeology
http://rome.classics.lsa.umich.edu/

Egyptian Artifacts Exhibit
http://www.memphis.edu/egypt/artifact.html

Megalythic Mysteries
http://easyweb.easynet.co.uk/~aburnham/stones.htm

Petroglyphs and Rock Painting
http://www.execpc.com/~jcampbel/

Resources on architecture include:

ADAM (the Art, Design, Architecture & Media Information Gateway)
http://adam.ac.uk/

The Ancient City of Athens
http://www.indiana.edu/~kglowack/athens/

The Bahaus
http://www.johnco.cc.ks.us/~jjackson/bauhaus.html

Gothic Dreams
http://www.elore.com/elore04.html

International Archive of Women in Architecture
http://scholar2.lib.vt.edu/spec/iawaspec/iawaguid.htm

Frank Lloyd Wright Foundation
http://www.franklloydwright.org/

Look into specialized subject areas to help students develop an interest in historical information. The history of aviation, for example, provides a great place to jump off into the study of history. Examples of sites you could start with include:

Airship and Blimp Resources
http://www.hotairship.com/

The Aviation History Online Museum
http://www.aviation-history.com/

History of Flight
http://tqjunior.advanced.org/4027/

The K-8 Aeronautics Internet Textbook
http://wings.ucdavis.edu/

National Air and Space Museum
http://www.nasm.edu/

Airship and Blimp Resources
http://www.hotairship.com/

The Aviation History Online Museum
http://www.aviation-history.com/

History of Flight
http://tqjunior.advanced.org/4027/

The K-8 Aeronautics Internet Textbook
http://wings.ucdavis.edu/

National Air and Space Museum
http://www.nasm.edu/

Science Methods

General reference and science gateway sites of interest include:

Cornell Theory Center Math & Science Gateway
http://www.tc.cornell.edu/Edu/

MathSciGateway/Explore Science
http://www.explorescience.com

Extreme Science
http://www.extremescience.com/index.htm

Frank Potter's Science Gems
http://sciencegems.com/

MadSci Net (Ask-A-Scientist)
http://www.madsci.org/

SciCentral
http://www.scicentral.com/

Science Education Gateway
http://cse.ssl.berkeley.edu/segway/

Scout Report for Science & Engineering
http://scout.cs.wisc.edu/report/sci-eng/current/index.html

Some of the science methods and general resources available on the web are:

Bill Nye The Science Guy!
http://disney.go.com/DisneyTelevision/BillNye/index.html

Biology4Kids
http://www.kapili.com/biology4kids/index.html

Chem4Kids
http://www.chem4kids.com/

Physics4Kids
http://www.kapili.com/physics4kids/motion/index.html

Science Learning Network
http://www.sln.org/

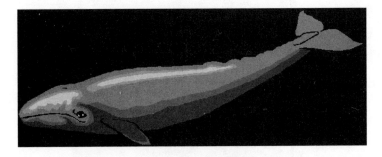

Whales: A Thematic Web Unit
http://curry.edschool.Virginia.EDU/go/Whales/

Information on Science Fairs can be found at:

Experimental Science Projects: An Introductory Level Guide
http://www.isd77.k12.mn.us/resources/cf/SciProjIntro.html

Reeko's Mad Scientist Lab
http://www.spartechsoftware.com/reeko/

Science Fair Central
http://school.discovery.com/sciencefaircentral/

Science Fair Project Resource Guide
http://www.ipl.org/youth/projectguide/

Science Fairs Homepage
http://www.stemnet.nf.ca/~jbarron/scifair.html

Step-by-Step Science Fair Success
http://www.accessexcellence.org/21st/TL/scifair/

Ultimate Science Fair Resource
http://www.scifair.org/

Useful biology sites include:

Surf Sites for Cyber Biology
http://ucsu.colorado.edu/~marcora/surf.htm

General Biology
http://www.schmidel.com/bionet/biology.htm

Ecology and Biodiversity
http://conbio.rice.edu/vl/browse/

Evolution and Behavior
http://ccp.uchicago.edu/~jyin/evolution.html

Information on science and health can be found at the following federal and international sites:

Centers for Disease Control
http://www.cdc.gov/

National Institutes of Health
http://www.nih.gov/

U.S. Department of Health and Human Services
http://www.os.dhhs.gov/

World Health Organization
http://www.who.int/

Some good gateway sites for animals include:

Birdwatching WWW Links
http://www.interlog.com/~gallantg/birdlink.html

Bill's Wildlife Sites
http://www.wildlifer.com/wildlifesites/

Zooweb
http://www.zooweb.com/

Specific animal websites include:

Birding Tips for All Seasons
http://www.birdwatching.com/birdingtips.html

Cat Fanciers
http://www.fanciers.com/

Canine Web
http://www.canine-connections.com/

Electric Zoo
http://netvet.wustl.edu/e-zoo.htm

The Complete Hamster Site
http://www.hamsters.co.uk/

Horse Web
http://www.horseweb.com/links/

Marine Mammals
http://www.mmsc.org/info/

House Rabbit Society
http://www.rabbit.org/

A Master Piece of Evolution—The Shark
http://www.ncf.carleton.ca/~bz050/HomePage.shark.html

Information on endangered animals can be found at:

Endangered Species
http://endangered.fws.gov/endspp.html

Endangered Species and Habitats
http://www.nwf.org/nwf/endangered/

Threatened Animals of the World
http://www.wcmc.org.uk/data/database/rl_anml_combo.html

For sources on the environment consult:

Environmental Protection Agency
http://www.epa.gov/

Environmental Organization Web Directory
http://www.webdirectory.com/

Greenpeace
http://www.greenpeace.org/

Population Index on the Web
http://popindex.princeton.edu/

Geology sites can be found at:

Geology Link
http://www.geologylink.com/

National Geographic Data Center
http://www.ngdc.noaa.gov/

U. S. Geological Survey
http://info.er.usgs.gov/

Mathematics Methods

There is a wealth of material available on mathematics on the web. Check out some of the following sites:

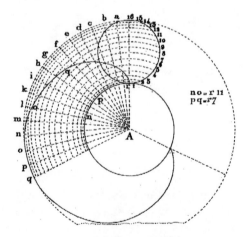

Ask Dr. Math
http://forum.swarthmore.edu/dr.math/

Geometry Through Art
http://forum.swarthmore.edu/~sarah/shapiro/

MathEd: Mathematics Education Resources
http://www-hpcc.astro.washington.edu/scied/math.html

Math Goodies
http://www.mathgoodies.com/

Mega Math
http://www.c3.lanl.gov/mega-math/index.html

On-line Mathematics Dictionary
http://www.mathpro.com/math/glossary/glossary.html

Space Exploration and Astronomy

An excellent gateway site for astronomy can be found at:

WebStars
http://heasarc.gsfc.nasa.gov/docs/www_info/webstars.html

For information on space exploration and astronomy, visit:

The Constellations and Their Stars
http://www.astro.wisc.edu/~dolan/constellations/

Exploring Mars
http://cass.jsc.nasa.gov/expmars/expmars.html

Galileo Mission
http://www.jpl.nasa.gov/galileo/

Mars Exploration

http://mars.jpl.nasa.gov/

Planetary Fact Sheets
http://nssdc.gsfc.nasa.gov/planetary/planetfact.html

Great activities to use in the classroom can be linked to at:

Amazing Space
http://wwar.com/

NASA Kids
http://kids.msfc.nasa.gov/

Chapter Five

Libraries, Books, and Literature on the World Wide Web

The World Wide Web is ideally suited for archiving and transferring large amounts of text resources. It is therefore no surprise that many of its sites focus on libraries, literature, electronic texts, and books. This chapter provides an introduction to some of these remarkable resources.

Exploring Library Resources on the Web

Many university and public libraries are making their catalogs available through the World Wide Web. It is almost certain that your university or college will have a major library web site and that you will be able to connect to it. In order to find the web address for your school's library, do a general search for your university's home page. Once you get to the home page, there will almost certainly be a menu item or link to your school's library.

You can use this approach to get to almost any major university library site in the country. You can also connect to library web sites through "nutball" sites. These are sites where some enthusiast on a particular subject has created as many links as possible to the subject.

"Nutball" sites that provide extensive links to public libraries with online services include:

Library WWW Servers
http://sunsite.berkeley.edu/libweb/

United Kingdom Public Libraries on the Web
http://dspace.dial.pipex.com/town/square/ac940/weblibs.html

St. Joseph County Public Library
http://sjcpl.lib.in.us/homepage/PublicLibraries/PubLibSrvsGpherWWW.html#wwwsrv

Other library sites that you might find interesting to explore include:

American Library Association
http://www.ala.org

The University of California
http://www.lib.berkeley.edu

Law Library of St. Louis
http://tlc.library.net/lla

Library of Congress Site
http://www.loc.gov

New York Public Library Home Page
http://www.nypl.org/

Portico—The British Library
http://portico.bl.uk/

University of Virginia Library
http://www.lib.virginia.edu/

College and University
http://www.mit.edu:8001/people/cdemello/univ.html

University of California Santa Cruz Campus
http://www.ucsc.edu/library/index.html

Literature

Many different web sites have been created to link to sources on literature. The following are some of the more useful:

The English Server
http://english-server.hss.cmu.edu/

Poems, Poetry, Poets
http://www.spondee.net/

Electronic texts can be found at many World Wide Web sites. Most are searchable, which means you can conduct interesting types of research using them. For example, suppose you decide that you want to write a paper on the use of the word *death* in the tragedies of Shakespeare. Going online would make it possible for you to find an electronic database where you could search for every place the word is used in his plays.

Probably the best source for electronic books is Project Gutenberg. The project currently has several hundred books available online in fully searchable format. You can find it on the World Wide Web at:

Project Gutenberg
http://promo.net/pg/

In order to search for electronic book resources online see:

Alex—A Catalog of Electronic Texts on the Internet
http://www.infomotions.com/alex/

Books Online—Authors
http://www.cs.cmu.edu/booktitles.html

Books Online
http://digital.library.upenn.edu/books/

The Internet Classics Archive
http://the-tech.mit.edu/Classics/index.html

Other valuable electronic collections include:

Bartleby Library
http://www.bartleby.com/

The Electronic Text Center at the University of Virginia:
http://etext.lib.virginia.edu/uvaonline.html

Internet Medieval Sourcebook
http://www.fordham.edu/halsall/sbook.html

Stanford University Digital Libraries Project
http://www-diglib.stanford.edu/

Resources on almost every specialized genre of literature can be found on the Internet and the World Wide Web. Poetry web sites, for example, can be found at:

British Poetry 1780–1910: A Hypertext Archive
http://etext.lib.virginia.edu/britpo.html

Electronic Poetry Center Home Page
http://wings.buffalo.edu/epc/

Lost Poets of the Great War
http://www.emory.edu/ENGLISH/LostPoets/index.html

Science fiction web sites include:

Linkhopping Science Fiction and Fantasy
http://sf.www.lysator.liu.se/sf_archive/sf_main.html

MIT Science Fiction Society Homepage
http://www.mit.edu:8001/activities/mitsfs/

Sources on critical theory and literature include:

Bakhtin Centre
http://www.shef.ac.uk/uni/academic/A-C/bakh/bakhtin.html

Boston Book Review
http://www.bookwire.com/bbr/bbr-home.html

Web resources on women writers include:

Women Writers Project
http://www.stg.brown.edu/projects/wwp/wwp_home.html

A Celebration of Women Writers
http://www.cs.cmu.edu/People/mmbt/women/writers.html

Guide to Women's Literature
http://www.facl.mcgill/ca/guides/women.html

Feminism and Women's Literature
http://www.andromeda.rutgers.edu/~jlynch/Lit/women.html

Censorship issues and banned texts can be found at:

Banned Books On-Line
http://www.cs.cmu.edu/Web/People/spok/banned-books.html

A good place to browse for interesting book titles is:

Book Browser
http://www.Polyweb.com/BookBrowser

If you are looking for specific book titles or authors, there are many references that you will find helpful on the Web. *Books in Print* is the standard library reference book for finding books that are currently in print. Online, there are many booklists with interesting links. Another method of finding what is currently in print is to visit the electronic bookstore Amazon Books, which has one of the largest collections of books for sale in the world.

Amazon Books
www.amazon.com

Barnes and Noble
www.bn.com

Book Wire Index—Book Awards
http://www.bookwire.com/index/book-awards.html

If you are interested in buying rare books online go visit:

Alibris
www.Alibris.com

Many major literary figures have web sites devoted specifically to them. You may find the following web sites useful for researching papers on individual authors or just to learn more about a particular author:

Jane Austen
http://uts.cc.utexas.edu/~churchh/janeinfo.html

Andre Breton
http://www.lm.com/~kalin/breton.html

William Burroughs
http://www.inch.com/~ari/wb1.html

Truman Capote
http://gopher.nypl.org/research/chss/spe/rbk/faids/capote.html

Raymond Carver
http://world.std.com/~ptc/

Willa Cather Page
http://www.courses.fas.harvard.edu/~cather/

Raymond Chandler
http://www.empirenet.com/~rdaeley/authors/chandler.html

Geoffrey Chaucer
http://www.vmi.edu/~english/chaucer.html

Arthur C. Clarke
http://www.lsi.usp.br/~rbianchi/clarke/

S. T. Coleridge Home Page
http://etext.lib.virginia.edu/stc/Coleridge/stc.html

Wilkie Collins Appreciation Page
http://www.rightword.com.au/writers/wilkie/

Emily Dickinson
http://userweb.interactive.net/~krisxlee/emily/

Rita Dove
http://www.engl.virginia.edu/faculty/dove.html

William Faulkner
http://cypress.mcsr.olemiss.edu/~egjbp/faulkner/faulkner.html

and

http://www.mcsr.olemiss.edu/~egjbp/faulkner/faulkner.html

Andre Gide
http://www.lm.com/~kalin/gide.html

James Joyce
http://www.2street.com/joyce/

Milan Kundera
http://www.georgetown.edu/irvinemj/english016/kundera/kundera.html

Doris Lessing
http://tile.net/lessing/index.html

Primo Levi Page
http://inch.com/~ari/levi1.html

The Jack London Collection
http://sunsite.berkeley.edu/London

The Life and Works of Herman Melville
http://www.melville.org

Walker Percy
http://sunsite.unc.edu/wpercy/

Alain Robbe-Grillet
http://www.halfaya.org/robbegrillet/

Anne Sexton
http://www.inch.com/~ari/words1.html

Shakespeare Web
http://www.shakespeare.com

Terry Southern
http://www.charm.net/~brooklyn/People/TerrySouthern.html

John Steinbeck
http://www.sjsu.edu/depts/steinbec/srchome.html

Robert Louis Stevenson
http://www.efr.hw.ac.uk/EDC/edinburghers/robert-louis-stevenson.html

The Tennyson Page
http://charon.sfsu.edu/TENNYSON/tennyson.html

Walt Whitman
http://lcweb2.loc.gov/ammem/wwhome.html

Chapter Six

Museum Resources on the World Wide Web

Many different types of museum resources are found on the World Wide Web. They can provide excellent sources for research in courses such as art history; European, American, and world history; and also for multicultural courses. Besides showcasing their collections, many museum web sites include curriculum materials and special activities for children and young adults.

Art Museums

There are many excellent general indexes and gateway sites for art museums that you can consult on the Internet. These include:

Art in Context
http://www.artincontext.com/

Art Museum Network
http://www.amn.org/

Art Museums on the World Wide Web
http://www.comlab.ox.ac.uk/archive/other/museums.html

Guide to Museums and Cultural Resources
http://www.lam.mus.ca.us/webmuseums/

MUSÉE
http://www.musee-online.org/directo.htm

Virtual Library Museum Pages
http://www.icom.org/vlmp/

World Wide Art Resources
http://wwar.com/

Resources on artists exhibiting on the World Wide Web can be found at:

Art on the Net
http://www.art.net/Welcome.html

For gallery and art resources, check:

Internet Art Resources
http://artresources.com

Virtually any type of art resource can be found at:

Worldwide Arts Resources
http://wwar.com

The Art Archive
http://artchive.com/core.html

A virtual museum can be found at the Web Museum in Paris:

WEBMUSEUM PARIS
http://sunsite.unc.edu/wm/

Almost every major American and European art museum has its own web site. Use them as a resource to learn more about individual collections or artists. Here is a list of some of the most interesting museums you can connect to on the web:

Alphonse Mucha Museum
http://www.webcom.com/ajarts/mucha.html

Art Institute of Chicago
http://www.artic.edu/aic/index.html

Asian Art Museum of San Francisco
http://sfasian.apple.com/

Banff Centre for the Arts
http://www.banffcentre.ab.ca/

The Brooklyn Museum
http://wwar.com/brooklyn_museum/index.html

Butler Institute of American Art
http://www.butlerart.com

Michael C. Carlos Museum/Emory University
http://www.cc.emory.edu/CARLOS

Marc Chagall Gallery
http://www.webcom.com/ajarts/chagall.html

The Detroit Institute of Arts
http://www.dia.org

Finnish National Gallery
http://www.fng.fi/

Florida Museum of Hispanic and Latin American Art
http://www.latinoweb.com/museo

Glenbow Museum
http://www.glenbow.org/

Guggenheim Museum
http://www.guggenheim.org/

Houston Museum of Fine Arts
http://www.mfah.org

The Kennedy Center's ArtsEdge
http://artsedge.kennedy-center.org/artsedge.html

Los Angeles County Museum of Art
http://www.lacma.org/

Lowe Art Museum (University of Miami)
http://www.lowemuseum.org/

Metropolitan Museum of Art
http://www.metmuseum.org

Minneapolis Institute of Arts
http://www.artsMIA.org

Montreal Museum of Fine Arts
http://www.mbam.qc.ca

Musee du Louvre
http://www.paris.org:80/Musees/Louvre/

The Museum of Modern Art, New York
http://www.moma.org/

National Museum of American Art
http://www.nmaa.si.edu

Palmer Museum of Art
http://www.psu.edu/dept/palmermuseum/

University of Memphis Institute of Egyptian Art and Archaeology
http://www.memphis.edu/egypt/main.html

Fine Arts Museum of San Francisco
http://www.famsf.org

Whitney Museum of American Art
http://mosaic.echonyc.com/~whitney

Famous Artists and Photographers

Almost every significant artist and photographer you are likely to find in an art history or photography course is likely to have information available about him or her on the Web. Here are individual sites for artists and photographers that you may find useful.

Ansel Adams—Fiat Lux
http://www.book.uci.edu/AdamsHome.html

The World of Escher
http://lonestar.texas.net/~escher/

Frieda Kahlo
http://www.cascade.net/kahlo.html

Claude Monet
http://www.columbia.edu/~jns16/monet_html/monet.html

Picasso and Portraiture
http://www.clubinternet.com/picasso

Diego Rivera Virtual Museum
http://www.diegorivera.com

Historical Museums

Historical museums not only provide valuable information on specific regions and specialized topics, but often broader historical background as well. If you are interested in learning about East Coast maritime history, for example, a visit to the Chesapeake Bay Maritime Museum will prove quite useful.

Chesapeake Bay Maritime Museum
http://www.cbmm.org/

If you want to learn about a topic such as Chicago during the Progressive Era, or the great Chicago Fire, visit the Chicago Historical Society.

Chicago Historical Society
http://www.chicagohs.org

Other interesting historical museums include:

Golden Gate Railroad Museum
http://www.io.com/~fano2472/ggrm

Henry Ford Museum & Greenfield Village
http://hfm.umd.umich.edu

Jewish Museum, New York
http://www.jewishmuseum.org/

Mariners' Museum, Newport News, Virginia
http://www.mariner.org/

Museum of American Frontier Culture
http://www.csvrgs.k12.va.us/Outreach/outreach_1st_grade/Frontier_Culture.html

Museum of American Political Life
http://www.hartford.edu/polmus/polmus1.html

Mystic Seaport Museum
http://www.mysticseaport.org/welcome.html

The National Museum of American History
http://americanhistory.si.edu/

Old Sturbridge Village Museum
http://www.osv.org

Science Museums

Many different science museum sites can be found on the web. Like art and historical museums, they are excellent sources of information on specialized topics, as well as rich resources for the development of curriculum materials. Science museum sites can also provide important opportunities for interdisciplinary inquiry.

Academy of Natural Sciences of Philadelphia
http://www.acnatsci.org/

Boston Museum of Science
http://www.mos.org/

The California Academy of Sciences
http://www.calacademy.org/

Carnegie Science Center
http://www.csc.clpgh.org/

Chicago Academy of Sciences Nature Museum
http://www.chias.org/

Explorit Science Center (Davis, California)
http://www.dcn.davis.ca.us/GO/EXPLORIT/

Fernbank Museum of Natural History
http://www.fernbank.edu/museum/

The Florida Museum of Natural History
http://www.flmnh.ufl.edu/

Fort Worth Museum of Science and History
http://www.startext.net/homes/fwmsh/

History of Science Museum in Florence, Italy
http://galileo.imss.firenze.it/index.html

Manchester Museum
http://museum.man.ac.uk/

Miami Museum of Science
http://www.miamisci.org/

National Museum of Science and Technology
http://www.science-tech.nmstc.ca/

Natural History Museum of Los Angeles County
http://www.nhm.org/

New England Science Center
http://www.nesc.org/

The New Mexico Museum of Natural History and Science
http://www.nmmnh-abq.mus.nm.us/nmmnh/dinosinnm.html

North Carolina Museum of Life and Science
http://triangle.citysearch.com/E/V/RDUNC/1000/09/78/8.html

Oregon Museum of Science and Industry
http://www.omsi.edu/

St. Louis Science Center
http://www.slsc.org/

Science Museum of Virginia
http://www.smv.org/

Science World (Vancouver, British Columbia, Canada)
http://www.scienceworld.bc.ca/frameset.html

SciTech Science and Technology Interactive Center
http://town.hall.org/places/SciTech/

The Smithsonian Institution, National Museum of Natural History
http://nmnhwww.si.edu

The Swedish Museum of Natural History
http://www.nrm.se/

University of Georgia Museum of Natural History
http://museum.nhm.uga.edu/MNHWWWintro.html

Chapter Seven

How Schools Use the World Wide Web

Schools at all levels of the educational system are setting up their own web sites. Nearly anything that can be done administratively or educationally in a school can be incorporated into a web site. Here are some of the types of information you will typically find at a school site:

- Background about the school, its address, key phone numbers, and the like.
- Information about the community.
- Teacher home pages including photographs, biographies, lesson plans, and so on.
- Student home pages, including personal essays, examples of written work, drawings, photographs, and the like.
- Special academic projects: results of experiments, international exchanges, field trips, essays, poetry, fiction, artwork, and the like.
- Extracurricular activities: clubs, literary magazines, yearbook, sports schedules and results, student government documents.
- Parent and community resources such as PTSA newsletters.
- School, community, and lunch calendars.

The best way to really get a sense of what schools are doing is to visit different sites across the country and even around the world.

Examples of School Web Sites

There is perhaps no better place to see the types of projects that are being done by schools using the Internet and the World Wide Web than to visit Web 66, a project sponsored by the 3-M Corporation and the University of Minnesota School of Education. Web 66 provides lists of the addresses of hundreds of schools both here and abroad:

Web66
http://web66.coled.umn.edu

The goals of the Web 66 project are:

1. To help K–12 educators learn how to set up their own Internet servers.

2. To link K–12 web servers and the educators and students at those schools.

3. To help K–12 educators find and use K–12 appropriate resources on the web.

Web 66 links to a series of very valuable home pages for educators interested in setting up web sites for their schools or in learning about what other schools are doing.

The Classroom Internet Server Cookbook is a great place to learn how to set up a web site for your school.

Classroom Internet Server Cookbook
http://web66.coled.umn.edu/Cookbook/Default.html

For an extensive list of school web sites at various levels of the educational system, as well as from around the world, Web 66's Internet Registry is outstanding:

WWW Schools Registry
http://web66.coled.umn.edu/schools.html

Setting Up a School Web Site

This book is too brief to provide you with an introduction to creating a school-based web site. If you are interested in pursuing this topic, visit the following sites, which should prove valuable.

Setting Up a Web Site for Your School: An On-Line Presentation
http://www.fred.net/nhhs/html2/present.htm

How Do They Do That with HTML?
http://www.nashville.net/~carl/htmlguide/

Internet in the Classroom Tutorial
http://www.indirect.com/www/dhixson/class.html

If you are interested in learning more about clip art the following sites provide a good start.

All Clip Art Site
http://www.allclipartsite.com/

Clip Art Central
http://clipartcentral.homestead.com/clipartwelcome.html

Clip Art Connection
http://www.clipartconnection.com/

Clip Art for Web Sites
http://www.graphicmaps.com/clipart.htm

For resources on using animations in web sites or in the types of backgrounds that can be used for a site, visit the following sites:

The Animated GIF's Library
http://www.arosnet.se/agl/

The Backgrounds Archive
http://the-tech.mit.edu/KPT/bgs.html

Information on protecting students online can be found at:

Safekids.Com
http://www.safekids.com/index.html

Various "filtering" programs that block students from inappropriate web sites include:

Cyber Patrol
http://www.cyberpatrol.com/

Net Nanny
http://www.netnanny.com/netnanny/home.html

SurfWatch
http://www.surfwatch.com/

In addition to child safety issues using the Internet, teachers, administrators, and parents need to set up guidelines for computer use in their schools. High school students visiting pornography sites is not a desirable use of computers in most schools, nor is vandalizing or breaking into someone else's site. Information on acceptable use guidelines can be found at:

Acceptable Use Policies
http://www.nmusd.k12.ca.us/Resources/Policies.html

Acceptable Use Policy Collection from Web66
http://mustang.coled.umn.edu/Started/use/Acceptableuse.html

Chapter Eight

Creating Curriculum on the Web

Many of the web sites included in this book provide excellent examples of how the Internet and World Wide Web can be used as educational resources. Visit these and other sites to begin to develop ideas about how you can use the web to develop your own curriculum units. In this chapter, you can further explore some of the ways the Internet and World Wide Web can be integrated into instruction.

This is a very large topic and can only be dealt with on an introductory basis in this chapter. Perhaps the most important point to be made is that the effective use of the Internet as a curriculum resource requires that its use be integrated into regular classroom lessons. While students may find it fun to "Surf the Net," doing so without a clear purpose, in terms of the curriculum, is a limited experience.

Therefore, the first and most important question any educator using the Internet and the World Wide Web has to ask is: How can this new technology improve instruction?

If, for example, you are teaching upper elementary school children how to write a letter, does an e-mail exchange with another school or foreign country help create excitement and interest in the project? Can it help students learn about other people at the same time, as well as about geography? I believe the answer is yes, that in fact, when properly used, the Internet greatly expands what the child can learn.

How you use the Internet and World Wide Web will depend on your curriculum and its objectives. Going online with your students will be of very little value if you have not carefully thought through your curriculum. Look at the lesson plan included on the following page. Adapt it for your own purposes as you develop strategies for your own curriculum units using the Internet.

WEB-BASED INSTRUCTION PLAN

PLAN PURPOSE/ OBJECTIVE(S)	
PLAN TOPIC/TITLE	
SUBJECT AREA	
GRADE LEVEL	
TIME ALLOTTED	
INSTRUCTIONAL CONTENT/ PROCEDURES/ TECHNOLOGY ACTIVITY	
INSTRUCTIONAL AIDS/ MATERIALS/ TECHNOLOGY RESOURCES	
PROCESSING/ ASSESSMENT/ EVALUATION	
SCHOOL DISTRICT CURRICULUM COMPETENCIES	
NATIONAL STANDARDS	

An example of incorporating the resources of the Internet and the World Wide Web with traditional curriculum can be seen in a recent project that the author of this book has completed with his colleague Charles T. Mangrum II for Curriculum Associates, Incorporated, called *Learning OnLine.*

Learning OnLine is a series of 16-page thematically oriented booklets on high-interest topics. These booklets make extensive use of resources found on the Internet and the World Wide Web. Targeted at the middle school level, the first three booklets in the series include *Apollo 11, The Wright Brothers and the Invention of Powered Flight,* and *Endangered Animals.*

Welcome to the Learning OnLine home page!

Learning OnLine is a program that will help you learn how to conduct research on the Internet's World Wide Web.

Not sure what the <u>Web</u> is? Click on a highlighted word to read its definition -- or just go straight to the Learning OnLine <u>Glossary.</u>

Using this Web site and your **Learning OnLine** books, you and your classmates can explore the far reaches of the <u>Internet</u> to find information about exciting topics such as space travel, the invention of powered flight, and endangered animals. As you do your research, you can use your <u>browser</u> to mark favorite Web sites with <u>bookmarks.</u>

Ready to get started? Click the hyperlink for the topic you want to explore. This will take you to the home page for that topic.

● *Apollo 11*

● *Endangered Animals*

● *The Wright Brothers*

Learning Online (Curriculum Associates)
http://www.curriculumassociates.com/LearningOnLine/

After introducing each student to the thematic topic of the booklet, a series of online explorations is undertaken in mathematics, social studies, and language arts. Using the Internet and resources found on the World Wide Web, students address high-interest thematic units as well as practical problems using information drawn from online inquiries.

Students using the curriculum go to a web site at the Curriculum Associates offices in Massachusetts and connect into a *Learning OnLine* home page. There, they are able to connect directly to web sites appropriate to the topic they are exploring.

The "Questions for Beginning Your Exploration" page in the *Endangered Animals* booklet, for example, looks like this:

Questions for Beginning Your Exploration

Find the answer to each question by using hyperlinks on the *Beginning Your Exploration* Web page.

1. Define each term. Give an example of an animal that fits each category.
    a. extinct species
    b. endangered species
    c. threatened species

2. What is the most important reason that animals are becoming extinct today? Why is this so?

3. Describe three ways in which humans are causing animals to become endangered.

4. Take the "Extinction or Survival?" quiz. Then check your answers.

Each of these questions is of high interest and requires integrating science skills and knowledge while making effective use of the Internet and World Wide Web. *Learning OnLine* is just one example of how the Internet and the World Wide Web can be integrated into traditional models of instruction.

Integrating the Internet into Traditional Curriculums

Here are some suggestions for how the Internet and the World Wide Web can be used in curriculum. They are intended only as starting points for thinking about how online resources can be integrated into traditional school curriculums.

1. Create e-mail exchanges for students.
2. Conduct comparative analyses via e-mail. (How much do certain foods cost at your supermarket? What is your weather like? And so on.)
3. Organize a scavenger hunt. (Have students collect information on topics from different web sites—a famous personality, an event in history, a city, and the like.)
4. Visit a newspaper like the *New York Times.*

5. Create an online newspaper.
6. Create an online gallery of links to famous works of art and the museums where they are housed.
7. Create an online tour of your community or school.
8. Track a stock.

9. Go on an electronic field trip to a major museum such as the Metropolitan Museum of Art, or visit an institution like the United Nations.
10. Create an online literary magazine.
11. Research a career.
12. Practice a foreign language via e-mail with a group of foreign students who want to learn English.
13. Study about an historical subject such as the Civil War by researching photographs at the Library of Congress.
14. Explore famous literary texts using electronic library resources.
15. Research a foreign country. (Create a report, write a report, assemble a bulletin board exhibit).
16. Participate in an international data collection project with scientists.
17. Talk to a scientist, author, or some other expert on a subject that is of interest to you or your community.
18. Create an historical timeline.
19. Explore traditional folklore.
20. Explore mythology.
21. Track the activities of a space shuttle launch.
22. Learn about a planet or astronomical phenomena.
23. Visit science museums, and explore specific topics like dinosaurs.

24. Explore a high-interest historical topic like the raising of the Titanic or the detonation of the first atom bomb.
25. Explore a topic like global warming or endangered animals.
26. Create a profile of your community.
27. Visit your local historical museum.
28. Explore a topic like the Holocaust.
29. Visit the White House.
30. Visit Congress, and track a pending piece of legislation.

31. Explore important documents in our history at the National Archives.
32. Visit a national park.
33. Study a favorite poet or writer.
34. Study population statistics from the Census Bureau.
35. Profile diseases like AIDS by visiting the center for Disease Control.
36. Explore health issues such as smoking and alcohol.
37. Learn about good nutrition.
38. Explore the work of a major architect like Frank Lloyd Wright.
39. Study the anatomy of different animals.
40. Conduct a study on human rights issues by visiting sites like Amnesty International.
41. Learn about weather patterns.
42. Create a list of great movies or books.
43. Create a list of books you would like to read or movies you would like to see.
44. Visit Mars online.
45. Learn about the history of computing.
46. Profile a famous person in science, women's history, or African-American history.
47. Lobby a political leader via e-mail.

48. Visit the Supreme Court.
49. Study a major Supreme Court case or a series of court cases (civil rights and desegregation, woman's rights, and the like).
50. Learn about a famous artist or photographer. (Create a bulletin board display, or report on them.)
51. Research a current rock star or television or movie actor.
52. Visit a web site about a hobby or collection.
53. Research an issue involving people's opinions by visiting a site like the Gallup Organization.

54. Explore the history of a Native American tribe.
55. Learn about different American minority groups by going online.
56. Explore gender equity issues by going to appropriate online sites.
57. Study a famous psychologist.
58. Explore a topic in special education like autism or deafness.
59. Share the collection and comparison of scientific data with classrooms elsewhere in the country.
60. Visit a web site concerned with human rights issues, and use what you find to create a class discussion.
61. Study the history of computing.
62. Compare the coverage of the news in an international paper like the *Jerusalem Post* with coverage of the same issue in an American newspaper.
63. Conduct a virtual dissection of an animal like a frog.
64. Learn about movies that have won an Academy Award.
65. Visit a television news site (ABC, NBC, CBS, and so on), and research a current event.
66. Explore issues involving computing and privacy.
67. Research a controversial issue like book censorship.
68. Learn about an art or craft like origami.
69. Create an historical timeline using Internet resources.
70. Collect together famous quotes for discussion using a source like *Bartlett's Familiar Quotations*.

71. Use different mortgage calculators to determine the actual cost of a loan.
72. Explore how the Internet and World Wide Web are changing traditional ways of communicating and exchanging information.
73. Become a member of a virtual community.
74. Learn about books that have been awarded major prizes like the Caldecott Award.

75. Use an online biographical dictionary or encyclopedia to write a biography about a famous person.
76. Use the Internet to explore sites about the weather such as hurricanes or *El Nino.*
77. Track legislation at the state or federal level.
78. Create an online gallery of personal artwork.
79. Create collections of graphic art that can be shared with and used by others.
80. Create an interactive map of your community or of a historic site that is of interest.
81. Learn about a traditional craft such as blacksmithing.
82. Visit a famous architectural site.
83. Learn about the history of the American flag.
84. Visit Ellis Island, and create a report on immigration.
85. Trace the history of a famous family or your own family.
86. Learn how to draw cartoons using resources on the Internet.
87. Study the history of dance.
88. Explore the history of games.
89. Study a famous composer.
90. Visit a zoo, and learn about different animals and how they live.
91. Learn about endangered animals and how they can be protected.
92. Study an ancient culture.
93. Learn about a favorite sport or sports figure.
94. Study an ethnic or religious celebration like Kwanza or Passover.

95. Learn about different utopian traditions (both historical and contemporary).
96. Explore etymology and the history of words and language.
97. Explore a public health policy issue such as smoking or wearing bicycle helmets.
98. Explore topics related to drug abuse and addiction.
99. Study a movement in art like surrealism or literary movements like romanticism.
100. Go online to learn about an ethical issue such as euthanasia or cloning.

Chapter Nine

Developing a Web-Based Educational Portfolio

Over the past decade there has been increasing interest among K–12 educators, as well as college and university instructors, in the use of educational portfolios. You may currently be developing a professional portfolio as part of your studies in education. If you are not familiar with the portfolio concept, think for a moment about an artist's portfolio.

An artist who puts together a portfolio—let's say, for example, a collection of drawings—is not only publicly presenting his or her work but also organizing and evaluating what he or she has done. The portfolio process should involve careful self-evaluation, reflection, and assessment.

An artist's portfolio also represents an act of creation, not unlike creating a book. There should a logic to a portfolio—a progression of work and ultimately a philosophy or point of view.

This chapter is intended to provide you with basic guidelines for developing an electronic web-based portfolio that demonstrates your competence and your personal work in terms of using the Internet and the World Wide Web as a teacher.

Electronic Portfolios: A New Idea in Assessment
http://ericir.syr.edu/ithome/digests/portfolio.html

You may question why this is necessary. I believe, as do professional groups such as the National Council for the Accreditation of Teacher Education (NCATE), that computer literacy and, more specifically, Internet and web based skills are a prerequisite for the next generation of teachers, or what NCATE refers to as the "New Professional Teacher."

The sophisticated use of computers by teachers—particularly the use of the Internet and the World Wide Web—will be a requirement for virtually every teacher entering the profession in years to come. This requirement will apply to teachers at all levels and in all fields.

Taking all of this into account, imagine for a moment being on your first job interview. It's at a school district in your hometown. You really want the job. It's perfect for you. The principal interviewing you notes that your grades are good, that you have gone through a good university program. She compliments you on strong evaluations for your student teaching, as well as examples of lesson plans that you have developed. She is also impressed by your recommendations.

The job is almost yours. But she has one more need. Her school makes significant use of computers in instruction. Each classroom has a computer linked to the Internet and the World Wide Web. Thematic web-based instructional units are widely used in upper grades. Students are involved in e-mail exchanges using the web, and they research their papers on it. Teachers in the school use computers for classroom management and record keeping, as well as for exchanging memos, scheduling, and so on.

The principal wants to know what your educational computing skills are—how you would integrate the Internet and the World Wide Web into your work as a teacher.

By presenting a web-based portfolio like the one outlined in this chapter, you could demonstrate your skills at the highest level, showing not only your ability to use computers and navigate the Internet and the World Wide Web but also to integrate them in meaningful ways into your instruction. Being able to do so could very well make the difference in whether you get the job.

Creating a Web-Based Electronic Portfolio

There are many elements that can go into an electronic web-based portfolio. If you are already developing a traditional educational portfolio, obviously nearly all of its components could be transferred over to an electronic setting by scanning in documents and editing statements of purpose, philosophy, lesson plans, and so on.

To create an electronic web-based portfolio that demonstrates your work in integrating computing and the Internet and the World Wide Web into your work as a teacher, you might want to consider the following suggestions:

1. Create an initial home page that identifies and anchors you and your portfolio. It can have a photograph of you or clip art that you think is relevant. Include your e-mail address or other appropriate ways to contact you. Include a brief biographical statement that outlines your academic work and field experience, as well as your professional aspirations. Make your statement fairly brief—no longer than two or three paragraphs.

2. Create a page with links to Internet Search Engines and tools you find particularly helpful.

3. Next include a statement of philosophy or purpose. This should reflect your views on educational computing and the use of the Internet and the World Wide Web for instruction.

4. Once you have created your statement of philosophy or purpose, create a menu of items for the portfolio. You may want to break this down in terms of subject areas that you have studied as part of your work in education.

5. Each section could include web-based lesson plans with relevant links. You can also include with each subject area links to what you consider to be valuable web sites in each subject area you have studied. These could include content area resources or sites with valuable lesson plans and materials.

Think of your education computer portfolio as a project in process that you can keep on developing as you continue your work in education. If your university does not support students publishing web sites, you can rent space on a server for as little as nine or ten dollars a month. You may even be able to find free space through various teacher organizations or even an Internet provider or service. When you start teaching, if your school has a web site, it is likely that you will be able to include your portfolio on a classroom or faculty site.

Also keep in mind that you can carry your web site around on a computer disk. If you go to an interview, you can insert your disk into a computer that has a web browser mounted on it and call up your site as a local file.

A good preservice teacher portfolio should demonstrate the creator's competence as a beginning teacher. A good strategy for organizing an electronic portfolio is to use state or national standards as an organizational framework for your document. In Florida, for example, the State Department of Education has established twelve "Educator Accomplished Practices" that all beginning teachers need to demonstrate. These practices include: 1. Assessment; 2. Communication; 3. Continuous Improvement; 4. Critical Thinking; 5. Diversity; 6. Ethics; 7. Human Development and Learning; 8. Learning Environment; 9. Planning; 10. Role of the Teacher; 11. Subject Matter Knowledge; and 12. Technology. Each standard can provide a major section for the organizing your portfolio.

If you don't want to use state standards, you can draw on the model standards for liscensing new teachers developed by the Council of Chief State School Officers as part of the Interstate New Teacher Assessment and Support Consortium (INTASC). These standards can be found at the following address:

Model Standards for Beginning Teacher Licensing and Development
http://www.ccsso.org/intascst.html

Online guidelines for creating a portfolio can be found at:

The Digital Portfolio
http://www.essentialschools.org/pubs/exhib_schdes/dp/dpframe.htm

Developing a Professional Portfolio
http://www.uwrf.edu/httpdocs/ccs/portfoli.htm

Networking with Digital Portfolios in Sharing Teacher Expertise
http://www.pedanet.jyu.fi/cato/study2.html

Electronic Teaching Portfolios
http://curry.edschool.virginia.edu/curry/class/edlf/589_004/resource.html

Examples of Electronic Portfolios (University of Virginia)
http://curry.edschool.virginia.edu/curry/class/edlf/589_004/sample.html

Creating Your Own Web Pages

Developing a web site is a fairly straightforward task. You may want to program in Hypertext Markup Language (HTML) or just use an editor. Editors can be found on most browsers, or you can purchase a web editor such as Microsoft Front Page, Net Object's Fusion, or Adobe Page Mill. It is not the purpose of this book to show you how to either program in HTML or use an editor. Be assured that the skills necessary to create your own web page are fairly simple.

You can also use a program like Microsoft's Power Point, create your portfolio as a Power Point Presentation and then convert it into a web site. This is easy to do. For more information on Power Point link to the following sites.

Microsoft Power Point
http://www.microsoft.com/office/powerpoint/

Exploring Microsoft Power Point
http://office.microsoft.com/features/AstPowerPoint.asp

Electronic portfolios can be enhanced by scanning in supporting documents (lesson plans, children's work from drawings to tests, and so on), as well by including photographs and even videos. Digital cameras make including classroom photos a relatively simple task, although care must be taken in most instances not to include identifiable pictures of students because of privacy issues.

In terms of creating your own web site, the following sites will help you get started. Your university may also provide introductory web programming instruction. The fact is that a couple of hours with a web editing program or manual will start you on your way without too much trouble.

Online Support Center
http://www.onlinesupport.com/

Web Page Design
http://www-3.one.net/explore/webpagedesign.html

Web/HTML Resource Page
http://www.webhaven.com/chen/webhtml

World Wide Web FAQ (Frequently Asked Questions)
http://www.boutell.com/faq/#intro

WWW Viewer Test Page
http://www-dsed.llnl.gov/documents/WWWtest.html

Chapter Ten

Using the Web as a Resource for Your Studies Outside of Education

Obviously the Internet and World Wide Web have significant resources that can help you in subjects outside of education. Many of the web sites already discussed in this book fit this category. In this chapter, I include other interesting sites that can be used in your college and university studies. The list does not cover all subjects, nor are all subjects covered as thoroughly or as completely as others. It is nonetheless hoped that it will be helpful.

General Humanities

Humanities (Galaxy)
http://www.einet.net/galaxy/Humanities.html

The Labyrinth
http://www.georgetown.edu/labyrinth/labyrinth-home.html

Sapphire Swan Dance Directory
http://www.sapphireswan.com/dance/

Music

Classical Music Composers
http://www.classicalmus.com/bmgclassics/comp-index/index.html

Classical Net
http://www.classical.net/

Classical MIDI Archives
http://www.prs.net/midi.html

Digital Tradition Folk Song Database
http://www.mudcat.org/threads.cfm

Musical Glossary
http://www.hnh.com/mgloss.htm

History

The Civil War
http://www.civilwar.com/

Civil War Letters
http://www.ucsc.edu/civil-war-letters/home.html

Gateway to World History
http://www.hartford-hwp.com/gateway/

History/Social Studies for K-12 Teachers
http://www.execpc.com/~dboals/boals.html

National Council of the Social Studies
http://www.ncss.org/

Social Studies
http://www.awesomelibrary.org/social.html

Foreign Languages

Eduhound Espanol
http://www.eduhound.com/espanol/defaultEN.cfm

ESL Games. Com
http://eslgames.com/

Language Links
http://polyglot.lss.wisc.edu/lss/lang/langlink.html

Parlez-Vous Francais
http://members.yourlink.net/kappa/espanole/french.html

Physics

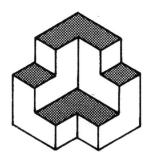

The Art of Renaissance Science
http://www.cuny.edu/multimedia/arsnew/arstitle.html

The Wonders of Physics
http://sprott.physics.wisc.edu/wop.htm

Astronomy

Adventures in Astronomy
http://www.mindspring.com/~thendrix/

Bradford Robotic Telescope Observatory
http://www.eia.brad.ac.uk/btl/

Comet Shoemaker
http://www.jpl.nasa.gov/sl9/

NASA Home Page
http://www.nasa.gov

NASA Kennedy Space Center (KSC) WWW Server
http://www.ksc.nasa.gov/

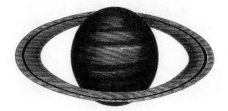

NASA's Planetary Photo Journal
http://www-pdsimage.jpl.nasa.gov/PIA

NASA Space Shuttle Launches
http://www.ksc.nasa.gov/shuttle/missions/missions.html

NASA World Wide Web Home Page
http://hypatia.gsfc.nasa.gov/NASA_homepage.html

The Nine Planets
http://seds.lpl.arizona.edu/nineplanets/nineplanets

Solar System Live
http://www.fourmilab.ch/solar/solar.html

Space FAQS
http://www.cis.ohio-state.edu/hypertext/faq/usenet/space/top.html

Space Telescope Electronic Information Service
http://www.stsci.edu

Biology

Biology Links
http://mcb.harvard.edu/BioLinks.html

Frog Dissection
http://curry.edschool.virginia.edu/~insttech/frog/

A Virtual Dissection of a Cow's Eye
http://www.exploratorium.edu/learning_studio/cow_eye/index.html

Virtual Frog Dissection
http://george.lbl.gov/ITG.hm.pg.docs/dissect/info.html

Chemistry

Chem 101 Home Page
http://library.thinkquest.org/3310/higraphics/index.html

Conversion of Units
http://www.chemie.fu-berlin.de/chemistry/general/units.html

The Learning Matters of Chemistry
http://www.knowledgebydesign.com/tlmc/tlmc.html

Treasure Trove of Chemistry
http://www.treasure-troves.com/chem/

Environmental Studies

The Daily Planet
http://www.atmos.uiuc.edu/

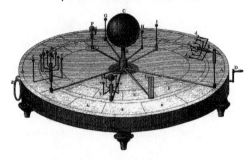

Rain Forest Action Network
http://www.ran.org/ran/

Earth Sciences

U.S. Geological Survey (USGS)
http://www.usgs.gov/

ElNet Galaxy's Pointers to Geosciences Resources
http://galaxy.einet.net/galaxy/Science/Geosciences.html

MIT Earth Resources Laboratory Home Page
http://eaps.mit.edu/erl/

Meteorology

Earth and Moon Viewer
http://www.fourmilab.ch/earthview/vplanet.html

Global Warming
http://www.ncdc.noaa.gov/ol/climate/globalwarming.html

NOAA (U.S. National Oceanic and Atmospheric Administration)
http://www.noaa.gov

The Weather Channel
http://www.weather.com/homepage.html

The Weather Unit
http://faldo.atmos.uiuc.edu/WEATHER/weather.html

Mathematics

21st Century Problem Solving
http://www2.hawaii.edu/suremath/home.html

Calculus
http://www.math.purdue.edu/~ccc/

General Math and Science Resources
http://www.tc.cornell.edu:80/Edu/MathSciGateway/

Geometry
http://www.geom.umn.edu/apps/gallery.html

Math Links
http://www.geometry.net/

MathMagic
http://forum.swarthmore.edu/mathmagic/index.html

The MathSoft Math Puzzle Page
http://www.mathsoft.com/puzzle.html

The Social Sciences

Social Science Data Collection
http://ssdc.ucsd.edu/ssdc/edu.html

Social Sciences Education (Galaxy)
http://galaxy.einet.net/galaxy/Social-Sciences/Education.html

Anthropology

Anthropology in the News
http://www.tamu.edu/anthropology/news.html

Oxford Institute of Social & Cultural Anthropology
http://www.rsl.ox.ac.uk/isca/index.html

Sociology

Bureau Of Justice Statistics
http://www.usdoj.gov.

Chapter Eleven

Other Topics of Interest

There are many reasons to use the Internet and the World Wide Web, including just for fun. It's also a good place to connect to games, learn about movies, and read the news or even plan a career. What follows is a list of interesting web sites you may enjoy visiting for any of the above reasons or just because you want to.

Just for Fun

Addicted to—Stuff
http://www.morestuff.com

American Philatelic Society
http://www.west.net/~stamps1/aps.html

The Aviary
http://www.theaviary.com/

Beer Can Collectors of America
http://www.bcca.com

Cat Fanciers
http://www.fanciers.com/

Children's Television Workshop
http://www.ctw.org

College Football Hall of Fame
http://collegefootball.org/

DC Comics Online
http://www.dccomics.com/

The Dilbert Zone
http://www.unitedmedia.com/comics/dilbert/

Disney
http://www.disney.com/

Dr. Toy
http://www.drtoy.com

The Freestyle Frisbee Page
http://www.frisbee.com/

Horse Zone
http://www.horsezone.com/

Joseph Wu's Origami Page
http://www.origami.vancouver.bc.ca/

Juggling Information Service
http://www.juggling.org/

The Museum of Advertising Icons
http://www.toymuseum.com/

Museum of Pez Memorabilia
http://www.spectrumnet.com/pez

Pets Connection
http://www.otn.com/ThePetPlace/

Professor Bubble's Homepage
http://bubbles.org

True Magic
http://www2.netdoor.com/~cowden/magic.htm

TV Theme Songs (& More)
http://themes.editthispage.com/

WWW Hockey Guide
http://www.hockeyguide.com/

Games

Game play and game-related sites include:

BU's Interactive WWW Games
http://www.bu.edu/Games/games.html

Interactive Games
http://www.nova.edu/Inter-Links/interactive.html

The Games Domain
http://www.gamesdomain.com

GNU WebChess
http://www.delorie.com/game-room/chess

Happy Puppy Games
http://www.happypuppy.com

The Movies

Film Zone
http://www.filmzone.com

Newspapers and News Services Online

Afro-American National News
http://www.afroam.org/information/news/current/news.html

AJR/News Link
http://www.newslink.org/

The Boston Globe
http://www.boston.com/

The Charlotte Observer
http://www.charlotte.com/observer/natwor

Chicago Tribune
http://www.chicago.trubune.com/print/news/current/news.html

Christian Science Monitor-International News
http://www.csmonitor.com

CNN Interactive World News
http://www.cnn.com/WORLD/index.html

The Jerusalem Post
http://www.jpost.co.il/

Los Angeles Times News
http://www.latimes.com/HOME/NEWS/

Newsday
http://www.newsday.com

The New York Post
http://nypostonline.com/

The New York Times
http://nytimesfax.com

USA Today Nation
http://www.usatoday.com/news/digest/nd1.htm

The Wall Street Journal
http://update.wsj.com/

The Washington Post-National
http://www.washingtonpost.com/wp-srv/national/front.htm

Magazines

The Atlantic Monthly
http://www2.theatlantic.com/

Business Week
http://www.businessweek.com

Life Magazine
http://pathfinder.com/Life

Mother Jones
http://www.mojones.com

Wired Magazine
http://www.hotwired.com/wired/

Television News Services

ABC News (Audio)
http://www.realaudio.com/contentp/abc.html

C-SPAN
http://www.c-span.org/

National Public Radio Online
http://news.npr.org/

World News Online
http://worldnews.net/

Television Networks

ABC
http://www.abc.com

CBS
http://www.cbs.com

Discovery Channel
http://www.discovery.com

NBC
http://www.nbc.com

PBS
http://www.pbs.org

Looking for a Job

CareerNet
http://www.careers.org

CareerPath
http://www.careerpath.com

CareerWEB
http://www.cweb.com

Conclusion

I hope this book will provide teachers with a brief introduction to using the Internet and the World Wide Web. It is intended to serve as a starting point for helping you to understand some of the possibilities inherent for teaching and learning by connecting to the Internet and the Web.

In many ways, introducing you to this technology is like providing an introduction to a library or telephone system. The quality of what you get out of a library will only be as good as the skills you bring to using it. Likewise, being able to communicate by phone is only valuable if you have something worth talking about.

The Internet and World Wide Web, whether as tools for research, teaching, or communicating with others, are ultimately what you make of them. I believe that the Internet has the potential to be the useful and exciting tool of our generation for teaching and learning.

Glossary

The following glossary will provide you with basic definitions for most of the computer, Internet, and web-related terms used in this book, as well as most terms you will need when you go online. For an online dictionary of computing technology visit:

Dictionary of Computing
http://wombat.doc.ic.ac.uk

Acceptable Use Policy (AUP): An agreement signed by students, parents, teachers, and administrators concerning the agreed-upon rules for using the Internet in a particular school.

Adaptive Technology: Adaptive technology is the use of computers—both hardware and software—to help challenged individuals overcome a limiting condition in their lives.

Alphanumeric: Pertaining to letters, numerals, and symbols.

American Standard Code for Information Exchange (ASCII): A common standard used in computer programs for converting 0s and 1s into letters of the alphabet, digits, and punctuation marks.

Analog: Continuous variable quantities such as voltage fluctuations, signals of a continuous nature that vary in frequency and amplitude.

Analog Computer: A computer that processes continuously variable data such as that created by voltage fluctuations. (*See* Digital Computer.)

Application Software: Software written for a particular purpose, such as word processing.

ARPANet: The ARPANet was a predecessor to the Internet funded by the Department of Defense.

Authoring Program: Software for coordinating the graphics, video, animation, text, and sound in the development of multimedia.

Backup: Copy of a file, disk, or program as a safeguard against loss.

Baud Rate: Refers to the speed at which a modem can transmit data. The faster the baud rate of a modem, the more quickly it can transfer information over a telephone line.

Binary Number: Information represented by 0s and 1s.

Bit: The smallest amount of data or information that is handled by a computer. In binary code, it is represented as either 1 or 0. Bits in groups of 8 are called bytes. Bytes can be used to represent different types of information, including numbers and the alphabet.

Buckley Amendment: The Family Education Rights and Privacy Act of 1974; legislation to safeguard students' and parents' rights to correct problems in the collection and maintenance of public records.

Bundled Software: Software that is sold with a computer, generally at a deep discount.

Byte: *See* Bit.

Calculator: Any device that performs arithmetic operations on numbers.

Cathode Ray Tube (CRT): The basic element used in a video terminal or television.

CD-ROM Drive: A device that reads the data from a CD-ROM into a computer. (*See* CD-ROM.)

Clip Art: Commercially available art and photographs that can be bought by users interested in incorporating them into their own projects.

Color Monitor: A color video screen that allows the computer to output graphical information—pictures, text, and so on.

Compact Disc Read-Only Memory (CD-ROM): CD-ROMs are aluminum disks coated with plastic that are "read" by a laser and have a storage capacity or over 600 megabytes. They are designed only to have information read from them and not to have information recorded on them. (*See* CD-ROM Drive.)

Communication Device: Any device used to enhance an individual's ability to communicate.

Computer-Based Training (CBT): Refers to training that involves special tutorials written for the computer. (*See* Computer Assisted Instruction.)

Computer Disk: A round, flat piece of plastic or metal coated with a magnetic material on which digital material can be stored.

Computer Literacy: The knowledge of how to use computers, including how to start and stop them and how to use basic applications and associated peripheral devices such as a printer.

Computer-Managed Instruction: A type of computer-assisted instruction that emphasizes management and evaluation programs, as well as instruction.

Copyright: The exclusive legal right to reproduce, publish, and sell the matter and form of some type of work.

Central Processing Unit (CPU): The main computing and control device on a computer; also called a microprocessor. Single-chip central processing units are used in most personal computers.

Cyberspace: According to the science fiction writer William Gibson, cyberspace is: "A consensual hallucination experienced by billions of legitimate operators in every nation, by children being taught mathematical concepts... A graphic representation of data abstracted from the banks of every computer in the human system. Unthinkable complexity. Lines of light ranged in the nonspace of the mind, clusters and constellations of data. Like city lights, receding..." Cyberspace has come to mean the place where data is transferred back and forth in our worldwide computer systems.

Database: A file or collection of data; a mailing list, a student roster, a grade sheet, or any of thousands of other similar collections of information or data.

Desktop Publishing: Involves the use of computers to create text and graphics for the production of pamphlets, newsletters, and books.

Digital: Pertaining to a single state or condition. A digital circuit controls current in a binary *on* or *off* state.

Digital Computer: Electronically stores information by representing information in two states, <u>on</u> and <u>off</u>, <u>+</u> and <u>-</u>, <u>0</u> or <u>1</u>. (*See* Analog Computer.)

Digitized Speech: Speech that has been recorded and converted to digital format to be used by computers and electronic communication devices.

Disk: A round, flat piece of plastic or metal coated with a magnetic material on which digital material can be stored.

Disk Drive: An electrical and mechanical device that reads and writes data to a disk. (*See* Computer Disk.)

Disk Operating System (DOS): This is any operating system that is loaded from a computer's floppy or hard drives when a computer is rebooted or started up again. MS-DOS refers to the proprietary disk operating system developed by the Microsoft Corporation.

Dot-Matrix Printer: A printer that creates characters by using a wire-pin print head. This is an impact device in which the wire heads strike a print ribbon like the keys on the typewriter. Dot-matrix printers are inexpensive and durable but do not usually produce printing with the quality of laser or ink-jet printers.

Electronic Bulletin Board: A place where people post messages and announcements that can be shared with others. Unlike e-mail, the messages are not addressed to a specific individual.

Electronic Mail (E-mail): A messaging system that allows Internet users to send messages back and forth much like the postal system.

Emulation: The use of hardware or software that permits programs written for one computer to be run on another.

File Transfer Protocol (FTP): Allows a user to be transferred across different sites on the Internet.

Firewall: A system that allows access to only some areas of computer systems to unauthorized users.

Floppy Disk: A mass storage device used mainly with microcomputers; made of flexible polyester film covered with magnetic coating such as iron oxide; designed to be removed from the machine and easily copied.

Freeware: Software that is given away free of charge. (*See* Shareware.)

Gopher: A menu-based system for searching data on the Internet.

Graphical Interface (GUI): Allows the computer user to run the machine by pointing to and activating a pictorial representation or icon shown the screen. Apple pioneered the use of graphical interfaces in educational and home computing. Windows is a graphical interface for DOS-based machines.

Graphics/Video Card: A circuit board that generates the video signal that appears on the computer's monitor.

Gutenberg, Johannes (c. 1400–1468): Credited with having invented movable type and the first modern printed book.

Hacker: A computer expert; person for whom extending the computer's capabilities is a consuming interest.

Hard Disk: Disks sealed inside machines with a large storage capacity (typically 1.6 to 2.1 gigabytes).

Home Page: A Web screen that acts as a starting point to go to multiple sites on worldwide computing networks.

Hyperlink: A highlighted graphic such as a button, illustration, or piece of text that connects a user to another web site or source of information or file on the Internet.

Hypermedia: Any combination of text, sound, and motion pictures included in an interactive format on the computer; an extension of hypertext emphasizing audio and visual elements. (*See* Hypertext.)

Hypertext: A model for presenting information in which text becomes linked in ways that allow readers to browse and discover the connections between different sets of information. (*See* Hypermedia.)

Hypertext Mark-Up Language (HTML): A coding system for creating hypertext links on web documents.

Icon: A specialized graphic image that represents an object or program that can be manipulated by the user.

Information Superhighway: Refers to the user being able to react to the computer through a command and have the system respond. This may be as simple as a user striking the wrong command and having the computer correct the user, or a user telling a computer to go in a certain direction in a virtual adventure game or simulation.

Ink-Jet Printer: A printer that sprays tiny drops of ink onto paper using an electrostatic charge; provides very high quality printing at a very low price.

Integrated Software Package: A collection of programs that work together to provide a user with multiple tool capabilities (word processing, spreadsheet, graphics, etc.).

Interactive: Refers to the user being able to react to the computer through a command and have the system respond. This may be as simple as a user striking the wrong command and having the computer correct the user, or a user telling a computer to go in a certain direction in a virtual adventure game or simulation.
Interface: The place where a connection is made between two elements. *User interface* is where people communicate with programs. *Hardware interface* is the connection between devices and components of the computer.

Internet: Successor to an experimental network built by the U.S. Department of Defense in the 1960s. Today it is a loosely configured system that connects millions of computers from around the world.

Joy Stick: A small boxlike object with a moving stick and buttons used primarily for games, educational software, and computer -aided design systems.

Keyboard: A device for imputing information into the computer; works very much like a typewriter keyboard but has a much wider range of capabilities.

Laser Printer: Uses the same technology as photocopiers to produce printed material. A focused laser beam and rotating mirror drum are used to create an image that is then converted on the drum into an electrostatic charge.

Liquid Crystal Display (LCD): A display that uses a liquid compound positioned between two sheets of polarizing material squeezed between two glass panels.

Liquid Crystal Display Projection Panel: Device that projects the contents of a computer screen via an overhead projector.

Local Area Network (LAN): Interconnected computers and related peripherals, such as printers and scanners, in one location such as a building or office.

Logo: A programming language designed for children by the MIT professor Seymour Papert.

Mailing List: In the context of e-mail, an electronic list of addresses; makes it possible for a single message to be addressed to many people at once. This function is particularly helpful when sharing information with a group--in getting people to work together on committees, and so on.

Mainframe: A high-level computer designed for sophisticated computational tasks.

Megahertz: A measure of frequency equivalent to one million cycles per second.

Microchip: A computer chip on which are etched the components of a computer's central processing unit.

Microcomputer: A computer that uses a single chip microprocessor.

Microprocessor: The main computing and control device on a computer. It is also sometimes called a *central processor*. Single chip central processing units are used in most personal computers. These devices can be thought of as the "brain[EFP, Jr.1]" of the computer.

Minicomputer: a mid-level computer whose capabilities are between those of a mainframe and a microcomputer.

Modem: An electronic communications device that allows a computer to send and receive data over a standard telephone line. The modem itself is an electronic device and is run by means of a communications program that is resident on the computer where the modem is installed.

Moore's Law: First formulated in 1964 by Gordon Moore. Moore, one of the cofounders of the computer chip manufacturer Intel Corporation, argued that the number of transistors that could be put on an integrated circuit would double every two years. The law has been modified and now maintains that the number doubles every eighteen months and increases fourfold every three years. Since basic prices for computers tend to remain constant, this means that the computer you bought 18 months ago can be bought for the same price today, only with twice the computational power.

Mouse: A pointing device that allows the user to input commands into a computer. (*See* Trackball)

Mud Object Oriented (MOO): Essentially a technically more sophisticated MUD.

Multimedia: The combination of sound, animation, graphics, video, and related elements into a single program or system.

Multiple User Dungeon (MUD): Imaginary adventure games resident on computer networks.

Musical Instrument Digital Interface (MDI): An interface that allows for the connection of music synthesizers, musical instruments, and computers.

Netiquette: The rules of proper behavior on the Internet.

Network: A collection of computers and peripheral devices that are connected by a communications system. Networks can be run in a small office or classroom or can operate on a worldwide basis. A *local area network* (or *LAN*) refers to a network that is run in a limited area such as an office, school, or campus.

Network Version Software: A software program specifically designed to run on a computer network where multiple computers or work stations have access to a single file server.

Operating System: Software that controls the computer and allows it to perform basic functions.

Optical Character Recognition (OCR): Computerized scanning technology that can interpret characters on the printed page.

Optical Scanner: An input peripheral that reads an image by reflecting light from its surface.
Password: A code word that lets one into a computer account; protects unauthorized use of an account.

Peripherial: Device such as a printer, scanner, or CD-ROM drive that is external to the computer. Data is passed between the computer and peripheral through some kind of cable.

Personal Computer: Another term for microcomputer.

Pixel: One dot on a computer's screen; the smallest element a scanner can detect or a monitor can display.

Platform: The foundation technology of a computer system.

Post-Typographic Culture: A post-modern culture.

Presentation Graphics: Systems designed for the presentation of visual and textual materials; primarily developed for business use, but have excellent classroom applications

Printing Device: Any one of a wide range of devices for producing a hard-copy version of a document, usually on paper.

Processing Speed: The speed at which data is manipulated within a computer.

Program: Software or the sequence of instructions that are executed by a computer.

Puff Switch: A type of computer switch input that is activated by sipping or puffing through a tube.

Random Access Memory (RAM): Information that can be read or used directly by a computer's microprocessor or other devices. (*See* ROM.)

Read-Only Memory (ROM): Refers to information or data that can be read by the computer but not modified or changed. (*See* RAM.)

Removable Hard Drive: A hard drive that allows its storage disk to be removed; very helpful when using large graphic or sound files that are very storage intensive.

Resolution: The clarity or detail of a monitor or printer.

Scanner (Optical): A device that uses a light-sensitive reader to scan text or images into a digital signal that can be used by a computer.

Server: A program or computer that is set up to provide users or clients access to files stored on a computer at a Web site.

Shareware: Software that is distributed for a free try-out, with users expected to pay the developer if they decide to use the software. (*See* Freeware.)

Simulation (Computer): Uses the power of the computer to emulate something in a real or imagined world.

Site License: Situation in which a software publisher agrees to make a software program available to be copied at a single site for a set fee. Such agreements are an excellent way to use multiple copies of a program at a greatly reduced rate.

Snail Mail: Name e-mail users have given to traditional, slower mail sent by the postal service.

Software: Runs the computer by giving it instructions to perform certain operations. A computer program is simply a set of instructions telling the computer to complete a certain task.

Sound Card or Board: An expansion board added on to a computer, which improves the computer's capacity to process sounds.

Speakers: Output devices that allow the computer to generate sound.

Spell Check: software that checks for spelling errors. Typically part of word processing software.

Spreadsheet: Application software that allows numerical data to be entered into cells arranged as rows and columns. Calculations can be performed on these data by entering formulas in appropriate cells.

Surge Suppressor: An inexpensive device for protecting computers from increases in the current of an electrical line.

Synthesizer: A computer device that generates sound from digital instructions rather than through manipulation of physical equipment or recorded sound.

Tape Drive Backup: An inexpensive device for making archive copies of a hard drive's programs.

Telecommunications Device for the Deaf (TTD): A device that allows individuals who are deaf to talk on the telephone by typing messages.

Telnet: Allows access to computers and their data bases, typically at government agencies and educational institutions.

Terminal: A device consisting of a video adapter, a keyboard, and a monitor where data can be input or output.

Touch Screen: An input device for computers that is activated by touch.

Trackball: Type of pointing device similar to a mouse. Unlike a mouse, it is stationary and can be used in areas with restricted space. (*See* Mouse.)

286, 386, 486 or Pentium based Computer: The different numbers that accompany the descriptions of most computers that refer to various types of microprocessors. The higher the number, the faster the machine. Pentium is the name used by the Intel Corporation, the main manufacturer of microprocessors, to identify their 586 chip. The microprocessor is the same as a Central Processing Unit or CPU. Modern microprocessors can contain over a million transistors in a chip that is only a square inch in size.

Typographic Culture: A culture or society that is based around the technology of printing.

Uniform Resource Locator (URL): An address for a web site. It tells your computer where the web site is and who is in charge of it.

User Friendly: Easy to learn and use.

Videodisc: A videodisc is a read-only optical disc that is used to store still pictures, motion pictures, and sound.

Virtual Reality: Refers to the idea of creating highly realistic simulations with computers. The most sophisticated of these simulations allow the user to manipulate objects and experience things (sex, walking through a museum, and so on).

Virus: A computer virus is a program that infects or corrupts other computer programs. An anti-virus program identifies virus programs and purges them from computer systems.

Web (World Wide Web; WWW): System providing access to Internet resources based on hypertext documents.

Web Browser: A graphical user interface that is used to view documents on the Web.

Web Page Address: The Universal Resource Locator (URL) for a particular World Wide Web Page.

Web Server: A web server is a computer on which a web site resides and which can be connected to through the Internet.

Web Site: A collection of documents found on a single computer.

Wide Area Information Servers (WAIS): These are computer servers that allow full-text keyword searches of information resident at sites on the Internet.

Windows: A multi-tasking software that creates a graphical user interface that runs on MS-DOS–based machines, introduced by the Microsoft Corporation in 1983.

Word Processor: A type of software program that makes it possible for a writer to write or compile text, edit, and revise what has been written, save what has been written and print it.

World Wide Web (WWW): A browsing system that makes it possible to navigate the Internet by pointing and clicking one's computer mouse; connects diverse sites by the use of hyperlinks.

Bibliography

Armstrong, Sara, *A Pocket Tour of the Kidstuff on the Internet* (San Francisco: Sybex, 1996).

Bailey, Elaine K., and Morton Cotlar, "Teaching via the Internet," *Communication Education*, April 1994, Vol. 43, No. 2, p. 159.

Borland, Candace M., "Arts EdNet: Arts Education Resources on the Internet," *School Arts*, January 1996, Vol. 95, p. 12.

Bowers, C. A., *The Cultural Dimensions of Educational Computing: Understanding the Non-Neutrality of Technology* (New York: Teachers College Press, 1980).

Cerf, Vinton G., "Networks," *Scientific American*, Vol. 265, No. 3, September 1991, pp. 72–81.

Cuban, Larry, *Teachers and Machines: The Classroom Use of Technology Since 1920* (New York: Teachers College Press, 1986).

Cummins, Jim, and Dennis Sayers, *Brave New Schools: Challenging Cultural Illiteracy through Global Learning Networks* (New York: St. Martin's Press, 1995).

Dertouzos, Michael L., "Communications, Computers and Networks," *Scientific American*, September 1991, pp. 62–69.

Dyrli, Odvard Egil, "Surfing the World Wide Web to Education Hot-spots," *Technology & Learning*, October 1995, Vol. 16, No. 2, p. 44.

Dyrli, Odvard Egil, and Daniel E. Kinnaman, "Connecting Classrooms: School Is More than a Place," *Technology & Learning*, May–June 1995, Vol. 15, No. 8, p. 82.
Dyrli, Odvard Egil, and Daniel E. Kinnaman, "Teaching Effectively with Telecommunications," *Technology & Learning*, February 1996, Vol. 16, No. 5, p. 56.

Dyson, Esther, *Release 2.0: A Design for Living in the Digital Age* (New York: Broadway Books, 1997).

Frazier, Gloria G., and Deneen Frazier, *Telecommunications and Education: Surfing and the Art of Change* (Alexandria, Virginia: National School Boards Association, 1994).

Harris, Judi, *Way of the Ferret—Finding and Using Educational Resources on the Internet* (Eugene, OR: International Society for Technology in Education, 1996).

Kelly, M. G., "Mining Mathematics on the Internet," *Arithmetic Teacher*, January 1994, Vol. 41, No. 5, p. 276.

Kirsner, Scott, "The Ultimate Web Master," *WebMaster Magazine*, October 1996. (electronic article off the web)

MacFarquhar, Neil, "The Internet Goes to School, and Educators Debate," *New York Times*, March 7, 1996, Vol. 145, p. C2, p. B1.

Meagher, Mary Elaine, "Learning English on the Internet," *Educational Leadership*, October 1995, Vol. 23, No. 10, p. 48.

National Council for Accreditation of Teacher Education, *Technology and the New Professional Teacher: Preparing for the 21st Century Classroom* (Washington, DC: National Council for Accreditation of Teacher Education 1997).

Office of Technology Assessment, Congress of the United States, *Teachers & Technology: Making the Connection*, OTA-EHR-616 (Washington, DC: U. S. Government Printing Office, April 1995).

Papert, Seymour, *The Children's Machine: Rethinking School in the Age of the Computer* (New York: Basic Books, 1992).

Papert, Seymour, *Mindstorms* (New York: Basic Books, 1980).

Provenzo, Eugene F., Jr., *Beyond the Gutenberg Galaxy: Microcomputers and the Emergence of Post-Typographic Culture* (New York: Teachers College Press, 1986).

Provenzo, Eugene F., Jr., *Video Kids: Making Sense of Nintendo* (Cambridge: Harvard University Press, 1991).

Provenzo, Eugene F., Jr., "The Video Generation," *The American School Board Journal*, Vol. 179, No. 3, pp. 29–32.

Turkle, Sherry, *Life on the Screen: Identity in the Age of the Internet* (New York: Simon & Schuster, 1995).